Pedagogy, Printing, and Protestantism

SUNY SERIES IN THE PHILOSOPHY OF EDUCATION
PHILIP L. SMITH, EDITOR

———————————————

Pedagogy, Printing, and Protestantism

THE DISCOURSE ON CHILDHOOD

Carmen Luke

State University of New York Press

Published by
State University of New York Press, Albany

For information, address State University of New York
Press, State University Plaza, Albany, N.Y., 12246

Library of Congress Cataloging in Publication Data
Luke, Carmen.
 Pedagogy, printing, and Protestantism : the discourse on childhood
 Carmen Luke.
  p.   cm. — (SUNY series in the philosophy of education)
 Includes index.
 ISBN 0-7914-0002-6.   ISBN 0-7914-0003-4 (pbk.)
  1. Education — Germany — History — 16th century.   2. Child rearing
 Germany — History — 16th century.   3. Printing — Germany —
 History — 16th century.   4. Printing — Social aspects — Germany.
 5. Protestant churches — Germany — History — 16th century.
 6. Reformation — Germany.   7. Germany — Church history — 16th century.
 8. Technology and civilization.   I. Title.   II. Series
 LA721.4.L84 1989   88-13924
 370'.943--dc 19   CIP

10 9 8 7 6 5 4 3 2 1

Woodcut on front cover is from Heinrich von Louffenburg, *Ein Regiment der Gesundheit Für die Jungen Kinder* (*A Regimen of Health for Young Children*), 1549 edition.

Contents

Acknowledgments

For their advice and criticism of the manuscript: Paul Delany, Kieran Egan, Allan Luke, Alec McHoul, and Anthony Wilden.

For their continuing support and encouragement: Haida Luke and Rhonda Hammer.

For typing the various versions of the manuscript: Joanne Pittard and Donna Eddleston.

This research was supported, in part, by Simon Fraser University, Canada and by James Cook University, Australia.

Introduction

In recent years, an increasing body of historical research has examined the social and ideological consequences of the advent of typography and the subsequent development of mass literacy. However, the direct and indirect influences of printing on pedagogy have been generally overlooked. In sixteenth century Germany, a new sensibility and attitude towards childhood emerged, reflected in the establishment of a state sponsored system of universal education. This is a widely overlooked concomitant of typography and the spread of print literacy. This book describes and explains how the relationship of printing, literacy, and early German Protestantism influenced the reconceptualization of childhood and pedagogy.

The history of childhood is a relatively new field of academic inquiry; researchers have sought data from diaries, autobiographies, children's toys, games or dress. Yet scholarship on the history of childhood remains sporadic and fraught with distortions and misinterpretations. Works on the history of childhood by P. Aries, D. Hunt, L. de Mause, E. Shorter, and others have been shown to be inadequate in their use of sources, methods of analysis, and conclusions.[1] My aim here is to provide a different approach to the study of the child in history by framing the object of study—childhood—as a study in the history of discourse.

In this book I do not make the child a focus of study. Instead, I examine how the child came to be a focus of study—an object of discourse—by way of analyzing historically concurrent, parallel series of discourses and practices. This enables the identification of a more extensive network of contributing influences to the formation of the early modern discourse on childhood than reference to categories such as education or history would allow.

In what follows, then, recent work in family and childhood history is reviewed. The early developments of the printing industry are examined, focusing on both secular and theological publications. The economic, social, and political conditions in Germany during the early 1500s are outlined to provide a context within which to situate the 1525 Peasant Rebellion and the subsequent educational reform movements. Luther's doctrinal disputes are discussed in relation to his conceptualization of the individual, his call for individual literacy and, hence, his promotion of public and compulsory schooling. School documents, popular literature, and Luther's theological tracts are analyzed to document the emergence of the modern discourse on pedagogy and childhood. Following Foucault, in order to situate a discourse and to locate the embedded object of study within it, one must search for links of opposition, juxtaposition or complementarity of concepts, ideas, and discursive practices in discourses historically adjacent and antecedent to the one under study. To consider the sixteenth century discourse on childhood only from the vantage point of "educational history" would provide us with an incomplete picture. However, by tracing Luther's theological justifications of the need for children's institutionalized education, we extend the investigation into the adjacent religious discourse. And in order to adequately account for the "spread of the word," historical archeology will necessarily lead us to consider the early history of printing. A survey of the dissemination of the new mass communications technology leads us to examine book publications which, in turn, returns us to discourses-in-print: the systematization, formalization, and circulation of ideas about childhood and childrearing.

Historians L. Stone, L. Pollock, G. Strauss, P. Greven, and K. Wrightson argue for a concept of the past as a gradual transformation, not an abrupt discontinuous history.[2] These authors reject the notion of a single evolutionary step in the history of the family — and by implication, the history of childhood — from the traditional, classical to the modern concept of childhood characterized by alleged bourgeois affection, permissiveness, and indulgence. Supporting a concept of historical change as gradual rather than abrupt, this study shows that even when new ideas or technologies emerge, social change accommodating and reflecting material or ideational innovation is gradual. Arguing against those historians who have accused parents in the premodern era of child abuse, neglect, a cruel inclination for infanticide and a general lack of interest in, indeed indifference towards the young,[3] I will show, as the records of the past reveal, that parents and "authorities" on childhood — pedagogues, moralists, and physicians—were not callously indifferent. What these authors have overlooked is a consideration of economic, medical, and social conditions that constrained the possibility of lavishing the kind of attention on children with which we are so preoccupied today. In the absence of detailed knowledge in the past about children's psychosocial and physiological development, we cannot point the accusatory finger at parents of the past for tying children to swaddling boards, tying them to apron strings, or hanging swaddled babies on wall pegs to prevent them from straying into hot ovens, falling into wells, riverbanks, or being attacked by domestic animals.

What is needed, then, is a more interdisciplinary and social theoretic approach to the historical discourse of childhood, one that seeks to uncover why ideas about children and technologies used on them changed. And, indeed, notions of childhood have altered significantly over the past five centuries. It behooves the researcher to uncover where and under what circumstances these shifts in attitude and childrearing practices came about. For the most part, childhood historians make claims about the evolution of the "Western family" and, by association, the child within an historical family based primarily on French and British sources. We take these generalizations then to stand for the "European family." Yet even within these broad binary distinctions—the Protestant British and Catholic French family—change occurred sporadically and unevenly, and lends itself even less to making generalizations about, say, the Polish, German, or Italian family. This book, then, addresses itself to making those historical and regional differences explicit by focusing on the German family in relation to the changing events and intellectual climate of the Protestant Reformation. These sociopolitical, economic and religious upheavals, in turn, are linked to the emergent technology of the printing press. By examining the circumscribing features of the early sixteenth century, we can identify the emergence of a dominant discourse on childhood and pedagogy.

Those looking for new historical data will not find it here; rather, traditional sources have been recast and juxtaposed in a discursive framework that situates the child in history in a context previously not considered by childhood historians. This study applies M. Foucault's method of discursive analysis to the uncovering of or, as he might have it, digging at the archeological site of the early modern concept of childhood. The framework of this volume is, then, by necessity interdisciplinary, drawing from historical discourses of several disciplines. In attempting to locate the historical emergence of the discourse on childhood, I have combined the discourses on the history of the family, pediatrics, printing, education, and reformation theology. I am aware that I have trespassed into disciplines without being able to claim the kind of knowledge and expertise expected of scholars in those respective fields. Nonetheless, I expect students and scholars of these (sub)disciplines of history to find this book instructive, informative and, at least, of curious interest, for, I fully expect to have raised several contentious issues by transgressing disciplinary boundaries. Such is the nature of an "archeological dig."

1

Pedagogy, Printing, Protestantism

Aims

This is a study in the history of an idea: the idea of childhood. The central aim of this book is to explain why and in what ways the concept of childhood changed from the "premodern" concept typified by alleged adult indifference towards children, to the early "modern" concept marked by increased and more systematic attention to children.[1]

Historians Aries, Stone, and Shorter argue that the shift from the premodern extended family unit to the modern nuclear family occurred over a three century period from 1500 to 1800. This book examines the first century of this period, when changing ideas about the family and children emerged in the literature of the Reformation. During the sixteenth century, there emerged in many European countries an entirely new body of literature concerned with the treatment of children at home and at school. Much of what was written about children was based on ideas derived from the authors of antiquity. But what was novel about this emergent discourse was an incorporation of humanist ideas and scriptural justifications for the methods and aims of childrearing. Pedagogues, moralists, pediatricians, and religious and educational reformers all advocated humane yet firm treatment for children; parents were admonished not to neglect the rod but also to love their children as God loved his earthly flock.

This is a study, then, in the emergence and development of a discourse — pedagogy — that expresses changing attitudes and ideas about children. Moreover, the rise of "pedagogy" is itself an emergent phenomenon in the history of ideas, and reflects a recognition that children were not considered as "miniature adults."[2] In contrast to Aries' claims of apparent medieval attitudes of indifference and ignorance about children, the late Renaissance period showed an increasing adult awareness of children as distinct social beings who developed characteristics and needs in identifiable stages.

There was an abandonment of the concept of the child as an immature adult, and his [the child's] emergence as a creature recognized as having special needs and aptitudes.[3]

Ideas about children and about their education did not remain in the sphere of academic, theological debate. That which was preached and printed was both in great demand by a literate lay public and, by the mid-sixteenth century, would form the basis for major, state-legislated educational reform.

What distinguished the sixteenth century discourse on children from that of previous centuries was the systematization of those ideas in print. It is not unreasonable to assume that the wide distribution of those ideas among a nonclerical reading audience of parents influenced, in perhaps unmeasurable ways, parental attitudes towards the young. The eventual implementation of the "new pedagogy" into social practice — the establishment of a universal and compulsory educational system — can be linked to the mass propagandizing of ideas made possible by print technology. Protestant reformers made optimal use of this through the printing and dissemination of standard textbooks, school ordinances, examinations, and record-keeping systems.

Foucault has noted that the manner in which ideas are organized or "systematized" is as important as the "content" of those ideas. In other words, an analysis of how ideas are conceptually or materially ordered, or of the rules that give select individuals or institutions the authority and right to "speak," provides, in Foucault's view, a better understanding of "conditions of possibility" for the formation, expression, and transformation of ideas, than analysis of the ideas themselves will allow.

> What counts in the things said by men [sic] is not so much what they may have thought or the extent to which these things represent their thought, as to that which systematizes them from the outset, thus making them thereafter endlessly accessible to new discourses and open to the task of transforming them.[4]

In order to explain, then, how and why certain ideas come about, equal consideration must be given to how those ideas are ordered, their mode of expression, the way new ideas oppose or are analogous to already articulated ideas, and which institutional or individual authorities sanction certain ideas. Yet the very historical medium for the "systemization" of ideas—what Foucault calls the "mode of expression"—is significant in constraining which ideas are articulated, by whom and to what effect.[5] Following this view, the development of Reformation ideas about children and education will be examined in relation to the then new medium of mass communication—printing.

Reformation historians have generally acknowledged the importance of printing as a new means for creating and disseminating ideas that greatly facilitated the rapid spread of Luther's revolutionary theology.[6] Compared to the slow and laborious process of hand copying manuscripts, moveable type enabled ideas to be mass reproduced and distributed faster and more efficiently. In contrast to the rate of transmission of ideas in an oral culture, the mass distribution via print of multiple and standardized ideas resulted in an accelerated public and political response to Luther's ideas—strong resistance in some regions, or broad support in others. Stone has noted, and most Reformation historians agree, that

> the main distinguishing doctrines of the Reformation were salvation by faith alone and the priesthood of all believers . . . . The key factor in the dissemination of these ideas was the printing press. . . . It was the printing press which disseminated at such speed the ideas of Luther, and the printing press which made that revolutionary document, the Bi-

ble, available to an unsophisticated but semiliterate laity. The result was the most massive missionary drive in history.[7]

Along with the diffusion of issues pertaining to doctrinal dispute and debate, ideas about the spiritual relationship between the individual and God via scripture, ideas about the social conduct and responsibility of the family, about marriage, children, the church, and the state, were simultaneously spread among the people. The "most massive missionary drive in history" was successful because Lutheran ideology was preached by pastors and itinerant evangelists in remote hamlets and villages, and because Luther's sermons also were available in print.

The early history of printing is an important factor in the development and course of Reformation events and ideas. However, the influence of printing on the spread of Lutheranism and the subsequent changes in the collective social consciousness must be considered in relation to antecedent and contemporaneous "landmark" events in human knowledge and experience. As H. J. Chaytor explains, the decades shortly before and after 1500 were marked by "significant events" in many spheres of human knowledge which, in retrospect, can be said to have changed the worldviews of literate men and women from a medieval to an early modern perspective.

> In 1492 Columbus made his great voyage, in 1494 Charles VIII invaded Italy, in 1500 Copernicus was lecturing in Rome, Erasmus and Luther were at work and in 1521 the Diet of Worms was held, while in the previous year Magellan has circumnavigated the globe. In the effects of such events the difference between medieval and modern is apparent, in the enlargement of outlook upon the world and the interpretation of man's [sic] place and powers in it. That extension of view would have unfolded much more slowly than it did, if the printer had not already been at work for half a century.[8]

Moreover, the recent interest in the advent of printing as a critical moment in the history of literacy has led to renewed research on the concomitants and consequences of printing.[9] Without print technology, as E. Eisenstein has noted, Luther could not have hoped to put a Bible in every household to promote "a priesthood of all believers." Universal public schooling could not have become a practical reality without the multiple duplications of text made possible by the press. The mass production of school tests and school ordinances enabled the wide distribution of specified knowledge and sets of institutional regulations.

Hence, public schooling would standardize what and how all children should be taught; it would provide all children with basic literacy skills and simultaneously facilitate the mass transmission of centrally selected and controlled knowledge. The organization of children in schools also would permit more systematic and uniform socialization; prolonged mandatory school attendance would provide an extended and legally sanctioned opportunity for school and church authorities to shape the attitudes, values, and beliefs of future generations. The uniform organization of schools, teachers, and students according to (textually) identical school ordinances distributed to all schools in pro-Lutheran territories and principalities eventually would have, or so Luther had hoped, a socially and religiously unifying effect on German society.

Thus, a central part of this analysis will examine how printing — its geographic expansion, book genres, censorship laws, publications, and distribution — influenced the dissemination of Lutheran ideology. Next, we will consider those aspects of Luther's theology that bear directly on the ideas he advocated concerning the family, education, and children. By linking the early development of printing with select theological and social aspects of Lutheranism, it will become evident that ideas about and attitudes towards childhood changed throughout most of the Protestant German society during the early and mid-sixteenth century as a consequence of the combined power of Luther's word in particular, and the printed word in general. As Eisenstein has noted, "that the new presses disseminated Protestant views is, probably, the only aspect of the impact of printing which is familiar to most historians of modern Europe."[10] I will attempt here to look "underneath" this commonly acknowledged relationship between print and Protestantism, and tease out a possible web of discursive relations that may have underlain the concurrent "rise" of Lutheranism, printing, and education in the context of the social, economic, and political milieu of the day. Mapping discourses in this way enables a more succinct identification, and a more comprehensive description and explanation of the range of influence that led to a change of the concept of childhood in sixteenth century Germany.

A History of Discourse

In *Discipline and Punish, Madness and Civilization,* and *The Birth of the Clinic,* Foucault traces the conceptual development of, and the rise of attendant institutions for the therapeutic confinement of the criminal, the "madman", and the ill.[11] The development of a formal discourse on pedagogy and the subsequent "birth of the school" follows patterns similar to those described by Foucault in his analyses of the development of the prison and its reform, the emergence of institutions for the mentally impaired and hospitals for the ill. In *Discipline and Punish*, for instance, he shows how, in France, the early modern concept of the criminal emerged during the eighteenth century as part of the discourse on penal reform. In the process of reevaluating existing penal institutions and ideas about criminality, justice, and punishment, a new practical and theoretical penal network was established upon which modern theories of law and crime were mapped. For example, newly defined taxonomies for identifying and describing criminal behaviors brought with them new civil laws of prohibition, and new forms of punishment; prisons were architecturally designed to both accommodate the classified criminal and to allow for the kind of surveillance large groups of classified individuals required. Those penal reformers who were instrumental in institutional and judicial reform created, and were themselves a part of, an emergent authority network of "warders, doctors, chaplains, psychiatrists, psychologists, educationalists."[12]

Documentation, or a "network of writing"—the archive of record-keeping—helped fix and verify offenses, judgments, descriptions of individual behaviors, identifications of rank, and locations of confinement; in other words "a 'power of writing' was constituted as an essential part in the mechanism of discipline."[13]

By documenting the series of "examinations" each individual was forced to pass through—from initial oral questioning at trials, to the recording of behaviors once institutionalized—record-keeping created a cumulative, individual "archive". Documentation and examination enabled amorphous "disciplinary power" to establish a "visible," that is, written and formalized, disciplinary code by which individuals could be classified, compared, identified, and defined. Printing enabled the "power of writing" to become universalized and standardized; teachers like wardens examined, evaluated, recorded, and described those in their charge according to standardized (administrative) forms based on underlying classificatory criteria. The distribution of printed (identical) forms to all penal (or pedagogic) institutions in a given region or district—regional would later become national—helped organize and order individuals, groups, and practices into a disciplined and orderly social body governed by the order of an emergent administrative discourse.

In schools, Foucault notes, similar processes of disciplinary organization were at work. And this study will show those similar patterns of development vis-á-vis the child: the emergence of a discourse on childhood and education at the beginning of the sixteenth century, the "birth of the school" at mid-century, and finally, the full institutionalization of the child by the close of the century. Notions of "rank," for instance, Foucault claims developed in the French educational order during the eighteenth century. Yet, criteria and methods for ranking the individual were specified in the Lutheran educational reform documents, the school ordinances, as early as the mid-sixteenth century. Rank defined

> the great form of distribution of individuals in the educational order: rows or ranks of pupils in the class, corridors, courtyards; rank attributed to each pupil at the end of each task and each examination; the rank he obtains from week to week, month to month, year to year; an alignment of age groups, one after another; a succession of subjects taught and questions treated, according to an order of increasing difficulty.[14]

Similar ideas about supervision, classification by examinations, confinement, or hierarchization, which underlay the eighteenth century French formation of institutional systems designed for therapeutic confinement (e.g., the prisons and hospitals), had already been articulated in the pedagogical discourse of sixteenth century German Protestant education. Indeed, Luther and pro-Lutheran educational reformers were very much concerned with the "proper" confinement and surveillance of the young—hence compulsory public schooling—and the classification of learners according to hierarchized abilities determined and certified by examinations.

The crucial role of "pedagogy—the book system, libraries . . ." formed "a whole stratum" of discursive practices and "institutional" supports in sixteenth and seventeenth century Europe.[15] In fact, the early "mass" educational systems constituted discursive practices that fixed youth into an institutionalized ritual focused on and derived from the ritualisation of the word:

> What is an educational system, after all, if not a ritualisation of the word; if not a qualification of some fixing of roles for speakers; if not a constitution of a (diffuse) doctrinal group; if not a distribution and an appropriation of discourse, with all of its learning and its powers?[16]

7

In analogy to Foucault's analyses of the emergence, definition and classification of criminality in eighteenth century France, and madness in the nineteenth century, his historical archeology of discourse can be applied to an analysis of the emergence of early modern pedagogy, schooling and changing definitions of childhood.

What, then, exactly is discourse? R. D'Amico explains that "discourse is a group of statements which have a regularity in the form of practice."[17] The statements within a discourse derive their meaning from "discursive practice." For Foucault, unless the statements of a discourse are considered in relation to a field of practice, such statements are meaningless, or "empty." Foucault explains that a discourse is based on the interplay of two axes of knowledge:

> on the one hand, that of codification/prescription (how it forms an ensemble of rules, procedures, means to an end, etc.), and on the other, that of true or false formulation (how it determines a domain of objects about which it is possible to articulate true or false propositions).[18]

Put in another way, discursive history studies both

> this interplay between a 'code' which rules ways of doing things (how people are to be graded and examined, things and signs classified, individuals trained, etc.) and a production of true discourses which serve to found, justify, and provide reasons and principles for these ways of doing things.[19]

Accordingly, I examine here both the prescriptions for home and school childrearing and discipline, and the theoretical formulations that justified and rationalized those practices which made childhood an "object" of study and of institutional practice circumscribed by discursive ("true") statements.

Concepts of childhood have not been studied as a history of discourse. The empirical history of education has been well researched and documented, as has the history of communication. Histories of the family and of childhood are still relatively new fields of inquiry, and much debate and controversy over regional and chronological aspects of change is evident.[20] It is from these discourses that I will draw the historical code(s) of prescriptions on how to raise and educate the young and draw out the corresponding ("true") discourse that served to rationalize those practices. This study attempts to contribute to the history of childhood by applying the methods of historical inquiry outlined by Foucault in the aforementioned works, to link the discourses of family history, educational history, intellectual history, and the history of communication in an effort to establish how the child came to be an object of study, an object of textual and practical discourses, and how these discourses conceptualized the child.

An examination of those institutions—the family and the school—which, in Foucault's words, "circumscribe" children's lives, will provide insights into historical prescriptions for childrearing practices at home and at school. Educational history, then, contributes to this analysis aspects of a formalized pedagogical discourse, and provides a sense of the discursive practices transmitted by schools to youth. From family history we can draw demographic and anecdotal information about less formal aspects of pedagogy: the training of children at home. Reformation ideas about children can be found in the secular literature of family conduct manuals, medical texts, popular literature, and in the reformers' theological tracts. And by reviewing the early history of printing, we can examine the early book trade in order to reconstruct the scope of the "spread of ideas" in general, and the circulation and formalization of ideas about children in particular.

Contemporary scholars of the history of literacy agree that book production is one of several indirect indicators of literacy.[21] In order to argue, then, that the advent of typography influenced a collective change in ideas about the family and childhood—by way of an increase in literacy concomitant with the rise of Protestantism—the expansion of printing and book production must be considered as one of several markers of change. As D. Cressy explains, print, literacy, and education must be viewed as historically concomitant phenomena:

> It is reasonable to assume some correlation between the level and progress of literacy, and book production, book ownership and the history of education. . . . The expansion or improvement of education increases literacy, which in turn leads to a greater demand for books. The rising output of printed matter makes it possible for more people to own books, and may itself stimulate the spread of literacy. The greater the circulation of books may create more opportunities for people to learn to read them.[22]

Cressy's comments reflect his particular findings on print, literacy and schooling in sixteenth to eighteenth century England. His methodological perspective, however, is shared by other social historians of literacy. The key word here is "correlation"—Cressy views print production as an indirect indicator of the advancement of literacy and is not arguing for a causal or linear relationship between the two. Graff also attempts to establish historical relationships among phenomena such as print, literacy, and schooling while avoiding an overestimation of the impact of print.[23] This study integrates their approach to the role of print as a potential "agent of change" and follows Foucault's notion of situating print within a "network of interrelations" which, through their interaction and interdependence, generate historical change.

The Reformation Background

The theological issues of the sixteenth century, in conjunction with the political, social, economic, and philosophical currents of the age, generated a religiously based protest movement that led to the institutionalization of Protestantism. The voluminous literature on the Protestant Reformation documents a variety of causes and consequences of the movement. The most commonly acknowledged causes are seen in the moral decline and disintegration of power of the Roman church in its internal authority structure, in its inability to maintain unity within Christendom, and in its entrepreneurial role as mediator between God and the people. A second, equally influential cause, first outlined by F. Engels, can be located in social and economic conditions.[24] Economic and political historians agree that a rising bourgeoisie and an increasingly impoverished peasantry and laboring class, in conjunction with a deteriorating economic situation of overpopulation and an inefficient, outmoded system of food production, led to mass support of Lutheranism by upper and lower classes alike, and ultimately, to the 1525 Peasant Rebellion.[25] The peasant revolt marked a pivotal point in the subsequent development of the modern German state and marked the onset of a more systematic formulation and implementation of Protestant ideas derived, in large part, from Luther's matured vision of a reorganized church and state order.

Another, more sociologically based explanation for the Reformation is, in Stone's words, "the rise of an educated elite of laymen" whose "growing control of the laity over the clergy is a phenomenon common to all stages of the Reformation."[26] According to Stone, the diminishing power of church authorities during the Reformation was, in part, due to the increasing influence of humanist scholars whose contributions to educational reform de-emphasized the training of professional clerics in favor of a classical education for the modern Renaissance individual. As well, vernacular translations of the New Testament undermined the authority of clerical mediation between believer, scripture and God.

From a study of Reformation causes, events and consequences to the study of tracing the development of an idea—the concept of childhood—one moves from a study of historical complexity to historical obscurity. For while the landmark events of recorded history—the wars, Reformation leaders, church ecumenical councils, the spread of printing, and so forth—serve as visible historical markers with which to reconstruct the development of Reformation ideas and events, the kind of social changes effected by "great events" and "great men" are more difficult to uncover since, at the level of everyday experience, changing attitudes, thought, and behaviors are generally absent from the formal historical record.

The reconceptualization of childhood was part of a much broader change in intellectual outlook. Central to the intellectual changes of the sixteenth century was the idea, held by orthodox Catholics and by Luther and his followers, that the church was in need of major reform. A major component of Luther's call for religious and social reform was the secular and spiritual redefinition of the family and of family relations, and, importantly, the need for total educational reform. These, for Luther, were fundamental preconditions for the reform of both church and state. The idea that the church could be reformed by establishing more effective means of recruitment than reliance on internal ecclesiastical promotion, also brought with it the recognition that a better educational foundation was needed for new recruits. For Luther, the need for well educated young people to assume leadership in the church and state was particularly important. Equally important, he initially considered universal rudimentary literacy as essential in enabling all people to have access to the words of scripture.

Religious questions in the sixteenth century were, by and large, political questions and vice versa. A unified church was considered a precondition for a unified state, and a unified state could support and protect one faith, one church. Hence, in order to promote and control uniformity of belief, a standardized educational system was seen as the best and most effective means of institutionalizing the young for an extended period of time. Under the controlled conditions of compulsory schooling, children—female and male—of all social classes in rural and urban areas could be brought under centralized surveillance whereby ideas could be uniformly transmitted and children's behaviors more closely monitored. Printed school textbooks and printed school ordinances distributed throughout the public schools and universities of reformed, pro-Lutheran territories enabled authorities to exert some measure of uniformity and control over what was taught and how it should be taught.

Perspectives on Historical Concepts of the Family and Childhood

Aries in *Centuries of Childhood* and Stone in *The Family, Sex and Marriage in England: 1500–1800* claim that ideas about childhood underwent change as part of the more profound 300 year transformation of the family.[27] As the title of Stone's work indicates, his study focuses on the English family, whereas Aries' work is a "social history of family life" in France.

Aries' central point, which is more fully discussed in chapter 2, is that childhood was "discovered" during the seventeenth and eighteenth centuries when adults recognized distinct differences between childhood and adolescence, for "until the eighteenth century, adolescence was confused with childhood."[28] The classification of adolescence as a distinct developmental stage, however, dates back to antiquity.[29] During the Middle Ages, according to Aries, young children "did not count," adolescents were considered as children, and early adulthood was considered "youth."[30] Until the mid-seventeenth century, infancy was seen to end at age five or six; between ages seven to ten children entered schools where all age groups mingled in the same class: "up to the end of the eighteenth century nobody thought of separating them."[31] Childhood and adolescence remained undifferentiated until eighteenth century middle class education established a system of age and grade related instruction.

Aries intends his study of past notions of childhood to be an account of European family history.[32] Yet as Stone's analysis shows, and as this study of sixteenth century Germany will show, from his predominantly French sources Aries has written a social-cultural history of the French family and French childhood only. During the sixteenth, seventeenth, and eighteenth centuries, Catholic France developed a very different educational system from Protestant England or Germany. In fact, the chronology of change in family structure, in education, and in ideas about childhood documented by Aries, corresponds to the same periodization of the eighteenth century that Foucault oulines as the critical juncture when the early modern concept of mental illness and criminality emerged in France. As Aries notes, the historically late childhood/adolescence distinction in France was due to the "tardy establishment of a connection between age and school class."[33] Again, Foucault makes a similar observation of the French educational order which he considers analogous to the organizing, disciplinary principles at work in French prisons and hospitals. Prisons sought to discipline the socially deviant, (mental) hospitals to restore (mental) health to the ill, and schools aimed to make the uneducated literate—to transform the unruly child into a disciplined adult. In each of these institutions, the classification and hierarchization of the clientele (e.g., surveillance corresponding the crime) and its symptoms (e.g., deficient literate competencies in the child) helped support the disciplinary regime of control over large numbers of individuals. And while the British and German educational system of the sixteenth century made age and grade classifications explicit, in France "this connection remained vague" in the sixteenth and seventeenth centuries.

> It will be noticed that the tradition of not distinguishing between childhood and adolescence, is a tradition which disappeared in the middle classes in the course of the nineteenth century, still exists today in France in the lower classes where there is no secondary education. Most primary schools remain faithful to the old practice of simultaneous tuition.[34]

Catholic and Protestant ideas about children and education followed separate chronological developments and should not be taken to reflect one unified transition in the "evolution of the Western family." A more thorough examination of the differences between sixteenth century Protestant and Catholic attitudes towards book learning, which I will show to have had conceptual and practical implications regarding educaton and children, is discussed in chapter 2.

Stone's ideas about changing concepts of childhood in England are more closely related to the situation in Protestant Germany. Change in British family structure, according to Stone, occurred between the mid-sixteenth and late eighteenth centuries. Whereas Aries' work is more of a study in cultural history based on sources derived from art and literature, Stone relates change in family life and structure to wider intellectual changes in religion, philosophy, and politics. And while, in Aries' work, the lack of quantitative data reflects his aversion to a statistically based explanation of family and childhood history, Stone incorporates, although he does not rely upon, demographic data to give the reader approximations of class differentiated marriage age, age at death, marriage durations, life expectancy rates, and so forth.

In agreement with Aries' view of the French family, Stone notes that, in sixteenth and seventeenth century British society, individuals

> found it very difficult to establish close emotional ties to any other person. Children were neglected, brutally treated, and even killed; adults treated each other with suspicion and hostility; affect was low, and hard to find.[35]

Stone's explanation for the development of such low affect in familial relations is as follows:

> the lack of a unique mother figure in the first two years of life, the constant loss of close relatives, siblings, parents, nurses and friends through premature death, the physical imprisonment of the infant in tight swaddling-clothes in the early months, and the deliberate breaking of the child's will all contributed to a 'psychic numbing' which created many adults whose primary responses to others were at best a calculating indifference and at worst a mixture of suspicion and hostility, tyranny and submission, alienation and rage.[36]

Another reason for such apparently low emotional tenor in the early modern family is seen to lie with the customary practice of prearranged marriage. Given the economic and political value and purpose of prearranged marriage contracts, emotional bonds, as we understand them today, were, in Stone's view, absent between husband and wife. And this lack of affect between parents was transferred to children, and other members of the family and community. Prearranged marriage, as Stone notes, did not come under criticism in England until the late seventeenth century. In contrast, prearranged marriage and lengthy betrothals had been vehemently rejected by Luther in his sermons printed as early as 1519. Moreover, Luther's pamphlets and popular literature called upon parents not to force their children into marriage and not to stand in the way of their children's choice of marriage partner.[37]

Stone's three-stage typology of the shift in family structure has some similarities to the development of the German family, but differs in its final stage. According to Stone's schema, the Open Lineage

Family existed from antiquity to the mid-sixteenth century; the Restricted Patriarchal Family "began in about 1530, predominated from about 1580 to 1640, and ran to at least 1700"; the Closed Domesticated Nuclear Family emerged in the late seventeenth century from the ranks of the upper bourgeoisie and squirearchy. The Closed Domesticated Nuclear Family was based on "personal autonomy," linked family relations by "strong affective ties," and saw the decline of patriarchal authority.[38] The latter development coincided with the emergence of the modern concept of childhood — one in which parent-child relations were based on love by both parents, where formal education was seen as necessary, and "among the wealthier members of society the new orientation towards children led to an active desire to limit their numbers in order to improve their life chances."[39]

The development in England during the 1520s of the Restricted Patriarchal Family is paralleled by a similar stage in family evolution in Germany. In the literature of the 1530s, at least, the importance of the family as the cornerstone of spiritual and civil harmony in the community is a recurring theme. Moreover, the necessity for good governance in the home was seen as the foundation for orderly rule in the state and church. Rule and order in the holy estate of matrimony increasingly became the responsibility of the *"hausvater"* whose role and status was conceived of as a secular reflection of the holy father's rule in the spiritual kingdom.[40]

Stone's model of the premodern Open Lineage Family, and the shift in the 1530s to the Restricted Patriarchal Family corresponds to similar chronological change in German thought about the family. Stone, unlike Aries, makes no generalizations about European history of the family and children. And if, for the moment, we accept that ideas about children changed over a period of three centuries in tandem with changes in the family which, in turn, can be linked to a variety of influences external to the family, the following becomes evident: that concepts of childhood changed unevenly and gradually across the social strata in a given society at different times in different societies and, furthermore, cannot be attributed to a single cause. The differences noted above between French, English and German education and childrearing practices indicate, in part, the kind of differences that the literature on the evolution of the Western family has generally neglected and, hence, obscured. This study is a contribution towards a more adequate distinction between those historical, social, and regional differences.

My premise is that Luther's reconsideration of the role, status, and nature of the human subject in relation to God, to the church, and to the state inevitably led him to reconceptualize aspects of the family and of childhood. The responsibility of parents and the role of the family in early childhood training were important issues for Luther. A morally sound upbringing in the home, balanced by discipline and love, was considered a fundamental precondition for effective formal schooling — effective in terms of benefits for the child, and success for the school system. In oral and printed sermons, Luther repeatedly stressed the need for harmonious relationships between husband and wife, and between parents and children in order to provide an emotionally secure environment for the young. For without parental moral guidance and affection, children would be unruly and undisciplined, morally and socially ill-prepared to learn in a classroom setting, and to obey school authorities and rules. A change in the concept and social relations of the Protestant German family in the first half of the sixteenth century predated similar changes noted by Aries in the French family during the late 1700s and early 1800s. I will argue, then, that the advent and expansion of print technology, the subsequent increase in secular and spiritual publications, and the spread of literacy converged with certain doctrinal aspects of Lutheranism which generated a fundamental shift in educational practice, and a change in attitudes and ideas about the family and childhood. In chapter 2, a discussion of the different attitudes towards printing, use of the vernacular, and literacy in France and Germany outlines historical possibilities that may differentially have influenced each country to develop educational practices and discourses about childhood at different times.

The Discourse on Childhood

Any study of children in history must, in the twentieth century, inevitably look at the ideas held by adults about children. Adult conceptions about childhood can be found by investigating childrearing practices which, in turn, historians have identified by examining the literature of educational history, children's literature, medical literature, autobiographies, or the representation of children in art and iconography. A study of children's games, toys or dress provides further insights into aspects of children's lives. Whether one looks to the literature, to art, or to the relics of children's toys or dress, one is necessarily confronted with adult notions about children. To study children in history, then, invariably means examining and interpreting adult practices and ideas that conditioned childhood experience. The history of childhood becomes a history of ideas, of institutions, and adult practices that circumscribe the child: the interplay of traditional and modern ideas, of methods of punishment and reward, of the ideas that informed how and where children were educated. The very ideas that children are objects of punishments and rewards, of rules, of education, of moral training, and so forth, constitute one knowledge axis: a code that prescribes procedures. And, since "practices don't exist without a certain regime of rationality," circumscribing the regime of practices are discourses that "justify, and provide reason for these ways of doing things."[41] In its totality, this interplay forms a discourse of practices and ideas that stipulate the role, status, and experience of children.

Young children in any era, unlike adults, do not have the cognitive or social maturity to evaluate, alter or resist the circumstances into which they are born. Not until adulthood is reached, and the necessary intellectual and social skill and status is acquired, can one enter and participate in the formal discourse of childhood. By the time the child has grown into a man—and we must recognize that, historically, participation in any formal discourse, particularly the discourse on pedagogy, was the domain of men—efforts to change or modify ideas about childrearing are from the perspective of the adult whose childhood memories have been mediated by time and experience. The pedagogical discourse—the ideas and practices advocated to train children at home and at school—is ultimately an insidiously powerful set of ideas and practices imposed on the most powerless segment of society: the young. In the absence of or with the support of institutionalized education, pedagogical principles and practices reproduce "silently" through generations, across societies, and over time. Importantly, the pedagogical discourse exerts itself with limited resistance from those on whom it is imposed. This silent reproduction of practices and ideas, then, comes to be seen as "natural."

Historical ideas about childhood do not always have a concrete referent in an idea permanently or systematically encoded in writing. The further back in history one reaches to trace the concept of childhood, the less documented evidence is available: as P. Laslett puts it, "crowds of little children are strangely missing from the historical record."[42] The most self-evident explanation for the paucity of sources is the historically diminishing chance of survival for historical records, particularly the chance of loss of manuscripts that are inherently more prone to destruction and deterioration than, say, architectural relics. Another explanation for the lack of historical commentary on children, and one which this study will, in part, address, is

Aries' point that children as individuals or as a social group have "not counted" in history.[43] That is, until the seventeenth and eighteenth centuries, children allegedly have been treated by adults with relative indifference, and therefore do not appear in the historical records of past eras. Children's omission from the historical narrative prior to the seventeenth century, which parallels the general absence of women from historical accounts and as authors, poses a number of problems for the reconstruction of past concepts of childhood. The omission of women and children in historical documentation leads to the perpetual rewriting of a history written by men, and seemingly lived only by men.

Discursive Authority: The Exclusion of Women and Children

Women and children, interestingly always found together in their exclusion as "non-men," have historically comprised a distinct group and subculture differentiated from and by men on the basis of age and gender. The biological imperatives of the reproductive process link mothers and children more closely physically, and to varying degrees emotionally, than fathers and children. It is not unreasonable, then, to assume that regardless of historically changing family relations or childrearing practices, women's commentary would undoubtedly contribute a perspective on children radically different from those formulated by men. Women's relative historical silence, however, leaves the historian to reconstruct past childhoods based on what men have observed, thought about, and considered significant enough to record. From the outset, then, we must recognize that the history of ideas about children, about women or the family, is a one-dimensional history: it is a history of the ideas men have held, ideas that men have reinterpreted and recorded over time, and ideas that men have imposed on themselves, on women and on children. That is, of course, not to suggest that economic or ecological necessity has not also influenced the development of certain ideas and social practices. Consider for instance the practice of child abandonment in times when and in regions where food was scarce; or the absence of ceremony at children's death or celebration at birth,[44] in times when infant mortality was high and death was a common occurence in all social strata brought about by famine, plague, inadequate nutrition, and sanitation.

Following Foucault's view on the discourse of history, women and children's exclusion from the historical discourse per se can be considered a "silent historical series" which of course, only becomes evident in retrospect. The absence of certain historical features — specifically, the omission of women and children — in the surviving records and in the secondary studies of history that were present of necessity, leaves us with a silent historical trace. And, since the trace — writing — is silent,[45] the absence of women and children in this double silence is ominous. As Laslett notes, "there is something mysterious about the silence of all these multitudes of babes in arms, toddlers and adolescents in the statements men made at the time about their own experience."[46]

According to Foucault, the formation or "manifest presence" of a given discourse is always in relation to other systematized sets of ideas or concepts. The manner in which a new or transformed concept emerges, then, is in juxtaposition to ideas already "enunciated" — that is, ideas organized within other discourses. He writes: The discourse under study may also be in relation of analogy, opposition, or complementarity with certain other discourses.[47] The absence of children and women from textual history, and in particular, the exclusion of women from the production of text has its analogy and its referent in the Bible, where concrete, textual evidence explicitly dictates the exclusion of women from the church. Hence, it follows that, historically, in a Judeo-Christian governed society, women would be generally excluded from public life, of which authorship for publication is only one aspect. In *The Policing of Families*, J. Donzelot comments on the "other" history of women:

> Thus beside, or rather beneath, the capital-letter history made by and for men there would seem to be another history, immobile and profound, linking the pyres where witches were burned alive to modern-day psychoanalytic couches for hysterics.[48]

The pedagogical discourse of the sixteenth century was derived from religious principles and assumptions and, hence, complemented, supported and diffused the dominant religious discourse in a broader system of ideas and practices that Foucault calls a "discursive constellation."[49] To explain children's appearance in sixteenth century discourse, one must look at, according to Foucault, such a constellation of adjacent and contemporaneous "networks of concepts", and how other discourses and the one under study are regulated and systematized. That is, one must search beyond that which is given and apparent in discourse, and look at how and why ideas are ordered as they are; how institutional systems and rules reflect those ideas they are designed to transmit; in what mode of articulation ideas are encoded (i.e., what system of documentation fixes and disperses ideas); what kind of political-judicial boundaries and social customs hold the practice of ideas within historical norms; under what conditions such boundaries are weakened at a certain time and place to enable new ideas and practices to break with traditional law or custom; what "authorities of delimitation" — individuals and institutions — have the right to reject or legitimate new ideas, and what historical conditions sanction their authority in the first place.

As will become evident in the course of this volume, those authorities of delimitation who cast a "network of power over childhood"[50] and who brought forth the child as an object of study by analyzing, explaining, defining, describing, and classifying the child by means of institutionalizing the young in schools were, indeed, men. That the history of ideas about children, as well as the history of education, is a history defined and written by men from antiquity to the present should be recognized at the outset. The absence of women's testimony to their own and their children's lives, childrearing practices, or household life, remains a recurring impediment to a fuller understanding of sixteenth century family life.

2

Approaches to the History of Childhood

THE history of childhood as a distinct disciplinary concern is relatively new. Until the early 1970s historical accounts of childhood
were subsumed under the general rubric of family history. Beginning
with Aries' seminal work *Centuries of Childhood*, published in 1960 in
France and translated into English in 1962, historical concepts of
childhood and childrearing practices have received increasingly
systematic study. Yet the concomitants and consequences of changing
ideas about childhood have been explained from differing perspectives, and the academic debate remains marked by much controversy
and dispute regarding the selection of sources, periodization, and influences on changing ideas about children.

Two approaches mainly characterize the study of the child in
history: What has come to be known as "social history", and what has
been more recently termed "psychohistory." The social history approach claims an interdisciplinary perspective, utlizing, inter alia, the

tools of demography, and the models of sociology and anthropology. Psychohistorians base their interpretations on psychological, psychoanalytic and, particular to the study of childhood, on developmental models.

Social historians of the family typically fall into two methodological categories; they are guided either by anthropological theory or a demographic-statistical approach. The assumptions underlying anthropological approaches are that the family is universal, that child-rearing practices are the link between the individual and society and, hence, that these socialization processes are central to understanding a given society. Rejecting the anthropologist's penchant for methodologically constructing a (causal) relationship between the nurture of children and a society's character, T. K. Hareven comments that anthropological theories which posit

> the typical family as a representative of the social order lack an analysis of the family as an institution reflecting class differences, population movements, and economic change. By treating the family as the microscopic representation of the social order, they fail to focus on the dynamics shaping family life and organization. The typology of a national character represents only the dominant culture, and leaves out the varieties of family experience among other groups in society.[1]

Demographic approaches to the history of the family generally focus on population changes, fertility rates, marriage patterns, literacy rates among household members, birth control practices, marriage age, infant mortality, and so forth. From statistical information, predominant fmaily structures can be identified and family functions, in terms of economic transactions such as landholding and inheritance patterns, can be isolated. Demographic data allow the historian to reconstruct, for instance, the distribution of economic or legal power within the family.[2] Psychohistorians charge that individual experience within the family, or the subtleties of relationships among family members, cannot be reconstructed by reliance on demographic data alone.

Socio-Cultural History

In contrast to the focus of demographic history on structural change or stability of the family, the socio-cultural approach to the history of the family emphasizes the need to trace historical change in attitude, meaning, emotions, ideas—in short, to write a *"histoire des sentiments."*[3] The "sentiments school" is represented by works such as: Ozment's *When Fathers Ruled*, Pollock's *Forgotten Children: Parent-Child Relations from 1500-1900*, Flandrin's *Families in Former Times*, Strauss' *Luther's House of Learning*, Stone's *Family, Sex and Marriage in England: 1500-1800*, Shorter's *The Making of the Modern Family*, and Aries' *Centuries of Childhood*. For my purposes, Aries' work is examined since it is the seminal work in the field of childhood history and one against which many studies, including this one, argue.

The central thesis of Aries' work is the "discovery of childhood" between the sixteenth and eighteenth centuries. During the Middle Ages and the beginning of the "modern era" (circa 1500), children, he claims, were not differentiated in a world of adults. Apart from infants' helplessness and physical dependency, Aries contends that there existed no separate realm of childhood. Children were considered "uninteresting," if not socially transparent; past infancy, they were seen as "miniature adults."

Aries furthermore argues that the discovery of childhood came about in conjunction with adult conceptions of a more extended developmental period between early childhood and young adulthood. Childhood was prolonged and the pubescent years were eventually classified as adolescence. Aries views this shift in adult attitude and corresponding childbearing practices pessimistically. The discovery of childhood created childhood and adult society where only society had existed before. The creation of childhood simultaneously separated children from adult society, limited their freedom among adults, and imposed severe disciplinary controls on children and youth by home, school, and church.

The main criticism of Aries by social historians is the alleged inadequacy of his sources. Aries' evidence for his arguments is drawn primarily from art and literature. His claim that no concept of childhood existed during the Middle Ages is justified by his explanation that children are absent from medieval paintings. Where children are portrayed, he argues, they are depicted as miniature adults in dress, physical features, and posture. In addition, as medieval historian B. Hanawelt has noted, Aries takes for granted that the medieval household consisted of both the extended family and outsiders who lived together under one roof.[4] P. Laslett rejects the notion of the dominance of the extended family during medieval times. In *Household and Family in Past Time*, he shows that the stem-family was not common in preindustrial England, but that a two-generational family structure predominanted. M. Anderson also suggests that England, northern France, North America, and the Low Countries had a low percentage of complex household patterns. Medieval household composition was not the same across Europe, or within one country. Moreover, Aries neglects to study the processes of childrearing before age seven, and justifies this omission by claiming that children "did not count" prior to age seven, the age at which children became economically productive.[5]

For psychohistorian DeMause, Aries' reliance on literary sources reflects a fundamental error of "mistaking books for life."[6] Yet Aries' intent was to write a cultural history of childhood, to show how adult attitudes and ideas about childhood changed in mid-seventeenth century France. And although Aries often loses sight of his stated aims and makes unsubstantiated generalizations to European history in general, he explicitly states in his introduction that "it is not so much the family as a reality that is our subject here as the family as an idea."[7]

That Aries' analysis is not substantiated by demographic data or autobiographical accounts is the main objection that DeMause, Anderson, and Stone have against his work. Strauss claims that he is "unimpressed" with Aries' argument that "death was tamed" in premodern times.[8] That is to say that parents, because of their alleged indifference towards children, took children's death in stride without much emotional involvement. Moreover, Strauss rejects as well Aries' claim of a late (nineteenth century) emergence of the concept of adolescence. Pollock, Ozment and Strauss disagree strongly with Aries' insistence that prior to the eighteenth century parents and schools set out to deliberately humiliate children.[9] Yet it is instructive to consider these criticisms in light of Anderson's point that:

> It has been becoming increasingly clear in recent years that many of the disputes in family history arise because different groups of scholars, even when apparently working on the same topic, are, often unconsciously, trying to write very different kinds of history and are thus adopting different approaches to the selection of problems for research, to the kinds of sources they employ, to the way evidence is and can be used, and to the relevance of social and economic theory to their work.[10]

On one hand, Aries insists that his is a study in the history of an idea; yet he also claims to have written a social history of the family which he does take to be representative of the development of the modern European family as a discursive object. Statistics alone do not provide sufficient evidence upon which to reconstruct family relations or the experiences of family members; yet reliance on literary or artistic sources also does not justify the kind of broad generalizations and explanations Aries uses to explain changing ideas about childhood.

A central problem in both Aries' and Stone's work, and one that seems inherent in medieval studies, is the lack of sources needed to justify claims about peasant life which historians tend to infer from evidence not derived from the peasant or laboring class. As Hanawelt notes:

> The approaches of peasants and the lower urban class to raising children were usually not represented in artistic and literary remains. For the Middle Ages the problem is particularly difficult because many of these sources were the works of ecclesiastical writers who had little direct experience with normal family life. Even the usual sources of information on childrearing in the Middle Ages are inconclusive.[11]

And so, both Aries and Stone offer histories of upper class family life; given that the literary remains of the upper, literate classes comprise the bulk of the sources the historian can consult, such data cannot, however, unequivocally be taken to reflect family life or childrearing practices across society. Stone's dismissal of Marxist analyses that attribute change in family type to industrial capitalism, reflects in the selection of his predominantly upper class sources; these sources support Stone's premise that the upper bourgeoisie, not the industrial proletariat, led social change by being the "first" group, educated and wealthy enough, to adopt new lifestyles.[12] Neither Aries nor Stone make clear that their sources are representative of an elite, literate minority only, which may or may not reflect family relations or childrearing practices of the society at large. Stone deals with the British squierarchy. Ozment's historical evidence is derived from the biographical records of a Cologne burgher and from the writings of Protestant reformers, moralists, and men in the "medical" professions.[13] Pollock insists that class — or education, culture, religious beliefs, or moral values — had no influence whatsoever on parent-child relations.[14] As if to reinforce her rejection of class as a possible influence of childrearing practices, she avoids working class testimony altogether. Neglecting to point out the limited applicability of their sources, these authors can easily mislead the reader to assume that the kind of evidence they provide is indicative of families in all social classes within a given society. The sources I cite in this book, similarly, provide testimony from a literate class only; I make no claims, however, about childrearing practices across the social strata, but, instead, provide the evidence on which to base claims about the existence of a formalized and institutionalized discourse on childhood.

Psychohistory

E. Erikson pioneered the application of psychoanalysis to historical inquiry in his biographical studies of Gandhi and Luther.[15] In later works, notably by Hunt and deMause, the insights of developmental psychology and psychoanalytic theory have been used to explain childhood and the family in past eras.[16] DeMause's anthology, *The History of Childhood*,[16] is the most representative work in the field of psychohistory since it draws together, for the first time, diverse psychohistorical research on childhood.[17]

Psychohistorians attempt to reconstruct the emotional tenor, the behaviors, and the psychological context of family life, within which children grew up. Intrafamilial relations are of primary concern, as distinct from the more traditional interests of historians: socioeconomic and political forces. Psychohistorical inquiry is typically guided by Freud's conception of developmental stages in childhood. These are considered to be universal and ahistorical features of human development. But do all children experience the kind of oral, anal, or phallic crises that Freud proposed? Discussing psychoanalysis and history, F. Halla comments on Stone's objections to psychohistory:

> First of all, Stone wants to know how an oral trauma develops when weaning occurs, as he suggests it typically did in premodern Europe, after libido energy has shifted focus to another erogenous zone? Secondly, where is the crisis reputedly connected with parental interference in and functions in a society that lived amid its own excrement . . . hardly ever washed, and whose women and children wore no underpants? How, thirdly, are we to impute crisis proportions to a "phallic stage" in the childhoods of individuals raised in home commonly devoid of even a modicum of privacy and in which sexuality was taken entirely for granted? And finally, since in most societies throughout history parents have perceived little need for an extended adolescence during which children

might spend several years preparing for adulthood, how is one to elevate a "crisis of puberty" to the status of a universal trauma?[18]

The heuristic aim of psychohistorical inquiry is the correlation of personality characteristics with generalized cultural characteristics. That is, the manner in which children are raised is seen to be the primary and fundamental influence on personality development; a generation of children raised in similar ways will reflect shared personality traits in a given society. Such a view does not make sufficient allowance for social class differences in personality formation; the labor and daily experiences among distinct social classes and ethnic groups do differ. These differences, in turn, must be seen to influence the values, beliefs, and attitudes that individuals develop throughout adulthood. These are transmitted to children and interact with another generation's social, economic, and cultural milieu, and individual experience. Moreover, the typecasting of a cultural personality according to childrearing practices, and vice versa, typically results in social stereotyping by "advanced" Western societies of "primitive" contemporary or premodern cultures that, for instance, do not toilet train the young. This phylogenic rationale for Western societal and intellectual development is based on a reading and extrapolation of an ontogenic first principle of individual development towards rationality. Such a view of the relationship between individual and societal development gives theoretic licence to claim for contemporary social organization a privileged historical position from which to point back along the historical path of "evolutionary progress"—back to the "dark" eras of an alleged unenlightened social primitivism and barbarism. According to B. Wishy, "attempts to link ostensible childhood experiences with a cultural style . . . [is a] limit peculiar to psychoanalysis" because

> considering the variety and amount of evidence psychoanalysis requires in the clinic just for understanding the individual case, what degree of information about nurture permits us comfortably to generalize about childhood and culture across the centuries, let alone from bizarre accounts of one child like the infant Louis XIII, as presented in the journal of Heroard, his physician?[19]

For DeMause, historical change—whether sociocultural, political, economic, or technological—comes about as a result of personality changes over time, which derive directly from changed child-rearing practices, that is, from altered parent-child relations. In his introduction DeMause presents his "psychogenic theory of history":

> the central force for change in history is neither technology nor economics, but the "psychogenic" changes in personality occurring because of successive generations of parent-child interactions.[20]

The possibilities for historical change, according to the psycho-historians, seem to lie, then, in the development of acquired characteristics. But perhaps the problem is one of social reproduction — not Freud.

A theory of history that bases explanations of change on the interaction of personalities over time has major drawbacks. One limitation of this approach is that it cannot account for those economic and social factors that mediate people's lives. Impoverished conditions may cause intolerable psychological stress in parents that may well lead to behaviors which, given our contemporary sensibility, would be categorized as excessive punishment, neglect, or child abuse. Also, in the households of the nobility, parent-child interaction may have been almost nonexistent as Hunt has shown in his study of Louis XIII, the French dauphin who was raised entirely by personal attendants.[21] As DeMause goes to considerable lengths to explain, generations of children were not systematically "raised" at all; until the eighteenth century

> the average child of wealthy parents spent his earliest years in the home of a wet-nurse, returned home to the care of other servants, and was sent out to service, apprenticeship or school by age seven, so that the amount of time parents of means actually spent raising their children was minimal.[22]

Anderson in *Approaches to the History of the Western Family: 1500–1914*, a review of current approaches to the economic and social history of the family, rejects psychohistory outright for the following reasons:

> One, which calls itself psychohistory and even has its own journal, the *Journal of Psychohistory*, seems already in its work on the family to have run into insoluble problems of evidence, and to have involved its practitioners in so much anachronistic judgement and blatant disregard for many of

the basic principles of historical scholarship, that I have not thought it worth detailed consideration here.[23]

DeMause's sources are primarily anecdotal accounts. Such personal observations reflect certain historical situations that delimit the experience of the writer and frame the substance of what was observed and recorded, and how. Anecdotal evidence does not fully account for those socio-structural or epistemic features that are "exterior" to the individual, that structure the kind of social world the individual records, and that constrain the interpretive possibilities by which people express their experiences in writing.

The ways in which people apprehend their environment is (pre)formulated by the statements about ideas, "reality," objects, facts, relations, and so forth that organize a particular field of reference. The human subject in any given historical era apprehends her or his world, the self, and the relations between self and others on the basis of historical discursive practices that name, locate and organize concrete and abstract knowledge and experience.[24]

In order to speak of things or objects, one is subject to the ways in which discourse has ordered them: an object is ordered conceptually in relation to other objects by being established in relations of resemblance, proximity, distance, transformation, and especially difference. These relations are established in discourse *and* between institutions, economic and social processes, behavioral patterns, systems of norms, techniques, types of classification and modes of characterization.[25] These relations are not inherent in the object (of study) nor do they reside within the observer — these relations "exist" discursively exterior to the object. Foucault suggests that these exterior relations are "what enables it [the object] to appear, to juxtapose itself with other objects, to situate itself in relation to them, to define its difference — in short, to be placed in a field of exteriority."[26]

How individuals apprehend, assign meaning to and interpret and record objects, processes, or events, then, is constrained "from afar" by rules and epistemic assumptions; these have their "ground" in discourses that govern, for instance, literary convention, religious discourse, the discourse of social folk-wisdom, and so on. These, in turn, stipulate the parameters of interpretation by which an individual comprehends her or his social environment. Thus, anecdotal commentary cannot fully account for the socio-structural and epistemic features, rule systems and fields of regularity that are, indeed, situated exterior to the individual, that guide thought, and that remain elusive to the individual in the presence of history. Anecdotal evidence does not explain how specific religious, political, cultural or epistemic features influenced and characterized discourse in the first place which, in turn, significantly influenced the ways in which people interpreted and assigned meaning to their experience.

The deployment of a "network of power over children" — whether to control their sexuality, education or upbringing — occurs not only in discourse but in institutions and everyday practices.[27] Conversely, the rearing of children is not everyday practice conducted in the privacy of the home exlcusive of external discursive reference to children's health, their education or morality. Without an historical, social, economic or even political context within which to situate childrearing practices, we are left with a history of childhood which "is a nightmare from which we have only recently begun to awaken."[28] It is little wonder, then, that DeMause's record is a history of battered children. He notes, for instance, that swaddling, tying children into restraint devices, and administering tranquilizing potions were widely practised, which kept children quiet, out of the way, and greatly reduced the time parents, that is mothers, spent with their children. DeMause reports that "opium and liquor were regularly given to infants throughout the ages to stop them from crying."[29] Infants opiated and immobilized by the bandages that bound them to boards could be "laid for hours behind the hot oven, hung on pegs on the wall, placed in tubs" and, generally, could be left alone for long periods of time. Once released from swaddling boards, infants were tied to leading strings to prevent their straying, strapped to backboards or iron collars to improve posture, or locked into immobile stool-like devices to control their mobility.[30]

Drugging, swaddling or tying up children, as DeMause claims, is "only one aspect of the basic aggressiveness and cruelty of human nature, of the inbred disregard for the rights and feelings of others."[31] To refute DeMause's blanket statement on the inherent cruelty of human nature, one might reasonably argue that restricting infants' mobility might have had survival and economic value when all able-bodied persons in a household were required to labor in the field and, hence, neither mothers nor older siblings were at leisure to lavish constant attention on the young. We might consider that, in the premodern era, the absence of the kind of contemporary fascination with the psychosocial aspects of child development so typical of our own time, and the absence of comprehensive knowledge of the physiological processes of growth, should temper our judgments of the motivations and practices of another era. Yet few of the authors in DeMause's volume "manage to find an occasional word of understanding or even support for swaddling or apron strings. Such sensitivity to complexity in the volume is regrettably thin."[32] The historian must exercise caution in imposing contemporary conceptual templates on past eras; we may hypothesize about the past on the basis of twentieth century theories but cannot make unequivocal claims. For instance, literature and politics, as Foucault observes, are recent categories "which can be applied to medieval culture, or even classical culture, only by retrospective hypothesis."[33]

To explain the behaviors, attitudes and feelings of adults towards children requires a broader sociocultural and historically grounded explanation than that which DeMause imposes on past parental actions: projective reaction, reversal reaction, and empathetic reaction. Historical change is not primarily the result of unrestrained impulses, projection or neuroses. Moreover, "deducing attitude, motive, wish, etc. from behavior was a problem before psychiatry presented it in new guise; and it endures."[34] DeMause's insistence that only "the psychogenic changes in personality" constitute "the central force for change in history" is as conceptually limited as are claims of technological or economic determinism.[35] And, while traditional history has given us accounts of a past marked by "great events" and "great men" who are devoid of emotions, family ties, childhoods, preferences, or aberrant behaviors, what is needed is a history that attends equally to the quality of everyday life of those people who participated in, and were influenced by great events and great men. P. Abrams in his discussion of the role of narrative in historical sociology comments:

> It is the problem of finding a way of accounting for human experience which recognizes simultaneously and in equal measure that history and society are made by constant, more or less powerful, individual action and that individual action, however purposeful, is made by history and society. People make their own history, but only under definite circumstances and conditions; we act through a world of rules which our action makes, breaks and renews — we are creatures of the rules, the rules are our creations; we make our own world — the world confronts us as an implacable order of social facts set over against us.[36]

Psychohistorians have made social historians aware of the necessity to consider the psychological aspects of family relations in history. However, overreliance on psychological justifications for historical change impoverishes any theory of history. And while most social scientists agree on the importance of early childhood experiences as formative for subsequent personality development, DeMause over-stresses the importance of childrearing practices as the "very condition . . . for the transmission and development of all other cultural elements."[37]

DeMause's aim is to introduce a psychogenic theory which might "provide a genuinely new paradigm for the study of history."[38] Rejecting the "century-long Durkheimian flight from psychology," DeMause proposes that psychological studies of historical parent-child relations will contribute to our understanding of why certain political or social forms, and technological changes emerged at different times in different societies. He hopes that psychologically based studies of history will

> encourage us to resume the task of constructing a scientific history of human nature which was envisioned by John S. Mill as a theory of the causes which determine the type of character belonging to a people or to an age.[39]

Attempts to scientize the history of human nature are conceptual constructs of this era. Such a view characterizes a set of historic epistemic assumptions aimed at rationalizing an organicist "mechanics" of individual and social development, and is an ethnocentric imposition of an historically specific epistemology on history and on an alleged human nature. We must consider whether the questions we ask of the present are justifiably asked of the past.

As Foucault has pointed out in *The Archaeology of Knowledge* and *The Order of Things*, intrinsic to the modern scientific discourses that emerged at the beginning of the nineteenth century, is the urge to scientize, totalize and unify human knowledge.[40] This need to explain and justify all human experience and knowledge according to precise and mechanistic rules, has led to the modern "episteme," which invests the human subject (human history, behavior, and knowledge) with a cause-effect rationality and with a progress principle, considered intrinsic to both the individual and society.

It is precisely this compulsion in the humanities and social scientific disciplines to unitize and periodize human experience according to notions of "progress of consciousness," "the teleology of reason," "the evolution of human thought," or "themes of convergence" that an "archeology of history" tries to circumvent.[41] Following Foucault's historical perspective, then, twentieth century social forms of organization are not in a state of "advanced" rationality in contrast to an earlier "irrational" age.

DeMause's call for a "scientific history of human nature" exemplifies this scientific compulsion to fix history and human nature in a closed system of cause-effect determinism, as J. S. Mill would have had it. Following Foucault, DeMause's historical model can be considered "a history that would not be a division, but development; not an interplay of relations, but an internal dynamic; not a system, but the hard work of freedom."[42] Once such a scientific "theory of the causes which determine the type of character belonging to a people or to an age" is established,[43] the link between our modern preoccupation with child care and development, and our discursively constructed Western cultural character, would (erroneously) justify our advanced political and social forms, and technological achievements as the pinnacle of human reason, progress, and rational development. Such a view casts each antecedent generation as progressively more unreasonable and hence irrational the further back in history one reaches. Wishy comments:

> If we were able to follow DeMause, we would look into the debates of the past for heroes and villains and put each age on trial for its contributions to the future happiness of children. This is not only an invitation to historical distortion, but rests on arrogance about our own time and its achievements for our century.[44]

Hunt's *Parents and Children in History* is another work in the field of psychohistory that attempts to explain both adult attitudes to, and the reality of childhood in seventeenth century France. His analysis of a seventeenth century journal is based on Erikson's developmental stage theory. To explain childrearing practices, parental attitudes and behaviors towards children, Hunt examines adult attitudes toward education. Yet adult attitudes are derived from Hunt's analysis of the journals of Heroard, the personal doctor-attendant of Louis XIII. The problem with Hunt's sources in terms of representativeness is obvious: What do the childrearing practices in the court of royalty tell us about middle or lower class children and parents in seventeenth century France? And while Hunt admits that "the list of sources has one obvious weakness: it tells us only about a limited segment of seventeenth century society,"[45] he then proposes that we can unproblematically extrapolate from the courtly concerns of raising a king to the lives of children of the common people. He writes:

> if the evidence shows that, even in this [royal] free and licentious atmosphere, sex was a source of anxiety and conflict for

both adults and children, it would necessarily follow that the same conclusion also applies to the rest of society, where mores were almost certainly more sober and conservative.[46]

Hunt's assumption that French society's sexual mores were "almost certainly more sober and conservative"[47] than those of royalty, is as vague and questionable as Aries' notion that a concept of childhood was absent from medieval consciousness because children were not realistically portrayed on canvas. Demographic historians reject such inferential leaps on the gronds that such a history "lacks precision over detail, timing and, above all, social class differences."[48]

Social-Demographic History

With statistical data of household composition, marriage rates, or inheritance patterns, "there is the problem of whether a knowledge of household composition always tells us the same set of things — or even anything very much — about familial behavior."[49] And too often, as Anderson notes, statistical data become "social facts," which are then qualitatively interpreted to explain family relations, behaviors, attitudes, and the quality of family life.[50]

Although no work exclusively concerned with the history of childhood has been written using the demographic approach, some of the more influential research into the history of children relies on existing family history, much of which is based on demographic sources.[51] And while lists, coroner's reports, wills or landholding deeds provide valuable information on household size, family structure or community composition, such data provide only limited insights into everyday processes of a given family or community. Anderson notes two fundamental limitations of the demographic approach. The first is a problem of meaning for the person who originally recorded events. He notes, for example, that a "problem would arise with illegitimacy, if there were changes or differences between areas in what was treated as a marriage and, therefore, in what was considered an illegitimate birth."[52] Admittedly, the family historian must work with those documents that have survived, but Anderson cautions of the "natural temptation to make inferences from demographic behavior to attitudes which may — or may not — have underlain it."[53] The second, more vexing and complex problem is the paucity of records for premodern times. And here the temptation to draw inferences from a limited data base is even greater than working with, for instance, seventeenth century documents.

Hanawelt illustrates how the problem of drawing monocausal inferences from a limited data base (coroners' inquests from the thirteenth to fifteenth century in Oxford, Bedfordshire and Northamptonshire) can be circumvented.[54] In her discussion of infanticide she acknowledges that "a fairly consistent pattern associated with infanticide is that female children were killed more frequently than male."[55] Yet the coroners' rolls of Northamptonshire revealed that the deaths listed as accidental for boys of all ages far outnumbered those for girls (63 percent boys; 37 percent girls). In the age group of one year and under, the usual age for abandoning or murdering infants, she found more boys listed under accidental deaths than girls. Hanawelt concludes, not with disproving claims about infanticide in general, or infanticidal trends for Northamptonshire in particular, but instead, offers possibilities:

> Concrete evidence for infanticide is still lacking. There are four possibilities: 1) infanticide was a widespread phenomenon but was accepted by society and, therefore, ignored in the records; 2) it was successfully concealed; 3) infant mortality being between 30% and 50%, willful murder was unnecessary; 4) all children were valued because of the need for laborers in peasant society of the fourteenth century.[56]

Similarly, when she reports that in her sample she found 50 percent of children under one year died in fires, and 21 percent died by drowning, she does not assert conclusions, but questions: Was this neglect or premeditated murder?

When interpreting demographic data, it is imperative that the historian relate statistical information with caution to statements about the quality or texture of life in the past. And even then, it will remain a difficult task to situate, conclusively, a given event within the very complex network of historical influences that directly and indirectly generate historical change. The complexity of influences that must be acknowledged in any history of childhood extend beyond the immediacy of the family. What must also be considered are the socioeconomic setting of the family, the political structure of the community, the geographic location of the society under study, the role of religion or education, and so forth. Moreover, historical relations between "institutions, economic and social processes, behavioral patterns, systems of norms, techniques, types of classification, modes of characterization" must be distinguished in order to fully account for "what enables it [the object of study: the child] to appear, to juxtapose itself with other objects, to situate itself in relation to them, to define its difference."[57] For these are essential contextual features which, according to Foucault, circumscribe communities, families, and children in historic-specific lifestyles, social customs, beliefs and values.

Centuries of Childhood: A Review

This section summarizes Aries' central ideas in *Centuries of Childhood* which still serves as a foundational work for all subsequent studies in the history of childhood. Recent studies have tended towards a more microhistoric focus, analyzing specific features in children's lives; Aries gave us an initial and a broad overview of, literally, centuries of childhood. He drew attention to the fact that children were absent from the formal historical discourse, that adults have held historically differing ideas about childhood which informed childrearing practices, and that childhood and the family must be an essential component in any study and understanding of society and of history. Most importantly, Aries raised questions about the treatment of children and the structure of the family, many of which he was unable to answer, but which have become the ongoing focus of inquiry for historians and social scientists. His work has inspired a generation of scholars dedicated to uncovering past childhoods and writing their history.

According to Aries, children in medieval society mingled freely in the adult world. The rich and poor, young and old were not institutionally or socially differentiated. Individualism, privacy or a formal work ethic were unknown.

> Work did not take up so much time during the day and did not have so much importance in the public mind; it did not have the existential value we have given it.[58]

Life was lived in public: in the streets, in the marketplace, in the fields, and on the roads. Aries sees medieval life as one of unrestrained freedom in the sense that the kind of institutional controls and regulations we know were absent. Aries rejects the traditional view of the medieval period which holds that religious morality constrained people's actions and behaviors. Instead, he pictures "a wild population . . . given to riotous amusements,"[59] Sociability typical of oral cultures marked medieval society, not the rigid piety of a moral and Christian way of life usually associated with the monastic, feudal image of medieval times.

In this riotous and raucous atmosphere children participated free-ly in everyday events:

> Transmission from one generation to the next was ensured by the everyday participation of children in adult life . . . where-ever people worked, and also wherever they amused them-selves, even in taverns of ill-repute, children mingled with adults. In this way they learnt the art of living from everyday contact.[60]

Aries distinguishes between "the infant who was too fragile as yet to take part in the life of adults" and, therefore, "did not count," and the child or "*enfant*". The "*enfant*" ranged in age from "late toddler" to early adolescence at which time children assumed full adult responsi-bilities: marriage or domestic service for girls, and apprenticeship at a craft or trade for boys. Notions of early childhood or adolescence, according to Aries, were nonexistent. It was not until the seventeenth century that the word "*bébé*" appears in French, borrowed, inci-dentally, from the English.[61]

Aries' suggestion that, during the Middle Ages, an "awareness of the particular nature of childhood" was lacking and that, in Hunt's words, "no detailed program for the raising of children" existed, re-mains questionable.[62] Recent works have argued against Aries' thesis of parental indifference towards the young in the premodern era[63] and his claims of an unbridled discipline descending on children at the ad-vent of the modern era. Stone's thesis of the loveless patriarchal fami-ly charactized by repression, discipline and unwavering obedience to the head of the household, comes under similar criticism to that level-ed at Aries. The current trend towards rectifying, or at least modifying the (mis)perceptions of historical parent-child relations as Aries and Stone have interpreted them, reflects in the recent works by Ozment and Pollock;[64] they argue that affective ties were never missing in the families of previous eras. For even without documented evidence, we can suppose that the basic techniques of infant care were surely passed on from mother to daughter throughout the ages; also, we can assume that someone took the time to teach toddlers that hearth fires are hot and dangerous, that hatchets and knives are not to be played with, or to stay clear of riverbanks and wells. There exists enough evidence in the literature of the sixteenth century to demonstrate that moralists, reformers, pedagogues, and pediatricians did, in fact, write 'detailed programs for the raising of children."

Towards the end of the Middle Ages, Aries sees a first subtle shift in adult conceptions of childhood. In the iconography of the thirteenth century, children begin to appear with more realistic child-like characteristics. In previous centuries, excluding Hellenistic art, "there are no children characterized by a special expression but only men on a reduced scale."[65] For Aries this suggests that,

> this undoubtedly means that the men of the 10th and 11th century did not dwell on the image of childhood, and that that image had neither interest or reality for them. It suggests too that in the realm of real life, and not simply in that of aesthetic transposition, childhood was a period of transition which passed quickly and which was just as quickly forgotten.[66]

By the late sixteenth and early seventeenth century, infants and children had become more visible and distinct in the French art and literature of the day; adult conceptions of childhood had become, according to Aries, more self-conscious. This new interest and change in attitude reflected in children's dress, games, toys, and a sudden rise in portrait paintings of children. The most profound change, however, was the dim recognition of differences between infancy, early childhood, and youth. Childhood was extended. Eisenstein, in her study of the impact of printing on sixteenth century society, appropriately notes an emergence of childhood a century earlier as the rise of a "distinctive youth culture."[67] And for Aries, this recognition of children as separate and different from adults marked the beginning of fundamental shifts in the lives of children. Children lost their freedom and were henceforth confined to the ever-increasing authority and discipline of French educational institutions: the college.

> Thus with the institution of the college appeared a feeling unknown to the Middle Ages and which would go on growing in strength until the end of the nineteenth century: revulsion at the idea of the mingling of the ages. Henceforth schoolboys would tend to be separated from adults and submitted to a discipline peculiar to their condition. . . . An important stage had been passed. The transition from the free school of the Middle Ages to the disciplined college of the fifteenth century was the sign of a parallel movement in the world of feelings; it expressed a new attitude to childhood and youth.[68]

During the sixteenth and seventeenth centuries, the very nature of the family changed: family ties became sentimental bonds and romantic love replaced medieval bonding that had stressed the importance of lineage and kinship links. By the late seventeenth century, the family began to turn inward; changes in architectural styles reflected the privatization of families from each other, and the individualization of members within families.[69] Moral reform, generated by the intensity and fervor of religious reform, imposed a social discipline unknown in previous centuries. Aries points to the rise of a new group of public servants and social managers—teachers in the schools, magistrates and jurists of the "law-courts", and police officers of the "police-courts"—who legally intercepted between the child and the social world, and between child and family.[70] Pedagogues assumed the role parents formerly held in supervising the young into maturity. And so, by the eighteenth century, Aries sees the break with the past as complete; the modern nuclear family had emerged, children had been institutionalized in schools, and society was transformed into an urbanized and highly organized economic and political apparatus.

Since the publication of Aries' book in 1962, numerous scholars have discussed and criticized his sources, assumptions and conclusions. These will not be reviewed here.[71] Chapter 2 will discuss those aspects of Aries' work that warrant further development and partially form the basis for the arguments in this study: a more precise, geographically differentiated explanation of sixteenth century features that influenced and contributed to changes in childrearing practices and changes in the family.

Aries claims that the sixteenth century growth in literature for and about children, and the concurrent transformation of the school into "an instrument of discipline" was a reflection of the way the adult population in general was changing its views on childhood. But as Eisenstein has pointed out, the dissemination of standardized knowledge made possible by the presses, enabled a minority—the moralists, reformers, humanists, and pedagogues—to influence the majority. We might question, then, whether the "growth in literature" and "the transformation of the school" was a reflection of a changed public attitude towards children, or if these changes were not a reflection of and instigated by a small group of literate reformers who, for a variety of personal interests, advocated change. Moreover, one might hypothesize that widespread dissemination of, and access to, the ideas of a few can change the opinions and viewpoints of a given social group; particularly if those ideas are financially and cognitively accessible—which the publication of inexpensive pamphlets and the use of the vernacular ensured. And if, as Aries notes, "the great event [in the history of childhood] was the revival at the beginning of modern times of an interest in education,"[72] then did this revival come from the hearts and minds of mothers and fathers, or was this revival not a result of the religious, moral, and political interests shared by an educated male elite?

A small group of men, notably Luther and his colleague Philip Melanchthon, Johannes Sturm, Martin Bucer, and Johannes Bugenhagen in Germany, Erasmus in the Netherlands, Thomas More, Dean Colet, and Roger Ascham in England, John Calvin and Huldrych Zwingli in Switzerland, and Saint Ignatius of Loyola, founder of the Jesuit order in France, wrote most of the sixteenth century formal educational literature. And while the bulk of the evidence resides in the reformers' documents which substantiate a restricted change in attitude towards children, or a "revival of interest in education," their testimony cannot be taken to reflect uniform attitudinal change across society. The whole notion of "change in adult attitude" should be qualified and delineated according to a more precise questioning of who brought forth new ideas about children and education, and for what reasons. What groups of discursive relations — epistemic, sociopractical, political, and so forth — interacted to construct the child as an object of study that would require observation, classification, certification, and discursive practices surfacing in the home and the institution of schools? What social processes transformed the ideas of a few, the "pacemakers" in Stone's words, to become mass opinion, or a shared perspective across the social spectrum in a given society? How influential was the new means of collecting, preserving, and disseminating knowledge and opinion? Did the fact that "books changed from being rare, costly, and unique to being plentiful, cheap, and standardized," foster a change in public attitude towards the family, children, and education?[73]

Mode of Expression: Coding Knowledge Relations

As I have noted, Aries located the rise of a discourse on childhood and youth in seventeenth century France. Stone, although not expressly concerned with the history of childhood or education, situates a shift in attitude towards children in England between 1660 and 1880. Aries sees the attitudinal change towards childhood as one marked by a "degrading discipline." Stone evaluates the eighteenth century change in attitude towards the individual and the family as one of warmth and autonomy as against the sixteenth century lack of intrafamilial affect. According to Stone, the "affective bourgeois family" of eighteenth century Britain cared enough for its offspring to limit their numbers so that fewer children would be emotionally and economically well provided for. This concern by parents with their children's welfare merged in the nineteenth century with greater industrial concerns over the need for a literate public: the need for mass public education. And while the more affluent sector would continue for the next two centuries to send their children to private schools, the rise of mass compulsory schooling is commonly, albeit wrongly, dated in the early nineteenth century.

What we have here, then, are traditional periodizations of significant historical events: the advent of mass education triggered by the productive needs of the industrial revolution, a change in attitude towards children as a consequence of the decline of social bonds based on kinship links, and the corresponding increase of importance placed on affective social relations. Stone further attributes these changes to the increasing power of the state over social and economic affairs previously the domain of the family, and to "the missionary success of Protestantism" that instilled morality into the majority of homes. Reconceptualizing holy matrimony and the home as a sanctified institution and site is seen as well to contribute to the new affect in domestic relations.[74]

Aries attributes the seventeenth century French change in attitude towards children to the newly emergent disciplinary regime of "magistrates, police officers and jurists." As these public servants increasingly influenced most aspects of private and social life, the child naturally would fall under their control: the school was transformed into an "instrument of discipline." Aries points to the state apparatus of control imposed on children as the cause for change in children's lives and attendant adult attitudes towards them. For Stone, the eighteenth century British aristocracy and gentry led the way for change in family life and, hence, change in the lives of children; class and culture, in Stone's view, underlay the shift from a premodern to the early modern concept of childhood.

In this study of sixteenth century Lutheran Germany, we will see that the religious and educational reformers of the Protestant movement dictated and legislated changing ideas about children and child-rearing practices. And, seeking to uncover what other relations, at the level of the more obvious historical markers, influenced a reconceptualization of childhood, I will take into consideration circumscribing power relations ("authorities of delimitation"), knowledge relations (dominant discourses, the production, dissemination and media of information), and sociopractical relations (the establishment and processes of schooling). Following Foucault, the "field" within which objects of study can emerge, in and by which they are assigned an identity, is ordered according to three levels of formation: (1) the surface of emergence, (2) the authorities of delimitation, and (3) the grids of specification.[75] Our guide, then, to uncovering possible connections previously not considered by scholars of family, childhood or educational history will be Foucault's threefold field of delimitation.

The "surface of emergence" is the site where an object first appears: the social, historical, political, cultural, or economic domain. Consider this analogy: the computer first surfaced in the political field of military intelligence for political-strategic benefits before it was co-opted by private enterprise for economic benefits; by subsequently resurfacing on the economic field as a commodity it rapidly has been consumed by and incorporated into the social field of home and work. We might continue and suggest that computers are locked into a struggle with traditional print on the epistemological field for dominance over the coding, storing, and distribution of knowledge: there is accordingly a correlative epistemological shift from humanist to technicist discourses.

The child in the sixteenth century emerged on the surfaces of the family and the school as well as in the domain of the religious-political discourse. Sixteenth century German religious discourse had not only to do with faith, sacraments, and prayer but also constituted political justifications for nationalism, military conflicts, monarchical alliances and, importantly, the break with papal Rome. As an object of discourse, the child, then, emerged in the epistemological domain of religion but, in historical retrospect, we can consider Renaissance religious discourse as political discourse as well.

Authorities empowered de facto and de jure to code and interpret knowledge are, according to Foucault, those individuals of professional rank usually associated with institutions. These controllers of knowledge are the "authorities of delimitation." Foucault considers both the individual(s) of rank within institutions and the (bureaucratic) institutions themselves as authorities of delimitation. Within such institutions as the penal system, the school, the church or government, individuals such as lawyers and judges, teachers, clerics, and administrators control and oversee the practices derived from and rationalized by the institutional discourse. These professionals are the same authorities who have the "right to speak"—the authority to construct meaning, to interpret, and to judge. The authorities who constituted the child in the discourse on pedagogy were, initially, Luther and his fellow religious and educational reformers, in the field of medicine the physicians, and in the field of popular literature the moralists. All subscribed to Lutheranism in one version or another and, therefore, to Luther's adoption of the Augustinian doctrine of original sin. As we shall see, instead of prescribing harsh treatment in the rearing of children to counteract innate sin, most childhood authorities advocated a firm yet loving parental hand in guiding children to maturity.

Foucault's third field of emergence is the "grid of specification." He writes that this category refers to "the system according to which different 'kinds of madness' [or any object of study] are divided, contrasted, related, regrouped, classified."[76] In other words, grids of specification are the ways in which the loci (e.g., the soul, the body, the mind, etc.) upon which discourse acts are divided, differentiated, classified, and so forth. The sixteenth century discourse on childhood laid the child on this grid: psychosocial development was conceived of in seven-year developmental stages; the soul was considered innately corrupt and sinful; the body — agent of the soul — was seen as enslaved to soul (and mind) and, therefore, the potentially most dangerous aspect of childhood and youth. Unless sinful tendencies were tempered early (following Saint Augustine, the mind could be filled with "good" sense impressions to counteract sinful ideas), and the child's body kept under close surveillance, depravity and immorality would rule the body: manifest in the behaviors and actions of the flesh. Moreover, such grids impose their own conceptual order on the object of study as it emerges in a particular disciplinary or practical field, and these historical grids are evident in the ways religious, penal, medical, or pedagogical authorities define the object. Psychopathology, as Foucault tells us, emerged between the space occupied by neurology and that occupied by psychology. Foucault notes that, in the case of psychopathology, it emerged as "a unity of another type, which does not appear to have the same dates [of origin], or the same surface, or the same articulation [as neurology or psychology]."[77]

A discourse and the object with which it is concerned emerge in between existing discourses, on uninscribed spaces, and the conditions and characteristics of their appearance are delimited by circumscribing discursive relations. These relations partially contribute to the formation of a new discourse and object yet also make claims upon them. New ideas, representations, practices may emerge with "borrowed" concepts, rules or practices from adjacent fields: psychopathological behaviors have descriptive and classificatory categories that resemble descriptions of deviant (criminal) behavior yet also have categories that can explain the same behavior via psychological concepts of mental derangement. So, new discourses bring with them transposed and/or modified conceptual baggage borrowed from existing discourses and yet, as new discourses become visible on a given field of emergence, surrounding disciplines make claims upon them: criminality becomes an object for the medical gaze. Knowledge of madness and its treatment is shared by the medical and psychological discourse with authorities on penal incarceration contributing expertise to the therapeutic and punitive confinement of the criminally insane. Such a "formation is made possible by a group of relations established between authorities of emergence, delimitation, and specification."[78]

Where, in the grid(s) of specification, then, did the child as an object of study within the pedagogical discourse emerge in the early decades of the sixteenth century? We are not looking for points of origin, but, rather, are looking for points of convergence, complementarity, opposition or parallelism in the range of knowledge relations and practices that may have contributed to the formation of the early modern pedagogic discourse. My claim here is that printing technology converged with the formation of early Protestant discourses on religious, social, and political reform. The child was an intrinsic component—an important object of attention—of these discourses since it was seen that the possibility for reform lay with the proper training of children. And because printing was such an essential part of the Protestant faith—mass distribution and consumption of ideas—the differences in attitude towards print between Protestant Germany and Catholic France may explain why the early modern discourse on childhood emerged in Germany in the early sixteenth century and not until the eighteenth century in France.

Returning, then, to our earlier question about the extent to which mechanized typography—the new mode of expression and means of collecting, preserving, and disseminating knowledge—may have contributed to the formation and formalization of the discourse on pedagogy, we turn now to a brief discussion of the early spread of printing and the different reactions to the press in Catholic France and Protestant Germany. For, as Eisenstein notes, the incentive to learn to read the Bible in the vernacular was inhibited for Catholics and encouraged for Protestants. By considering the implications for children and their education of the differences between the two nations—one encouraging printers, publishing, the vernacular and reading, the other censoring the new book-learning—we may be able to identify a relationship between printing and geographic and historical differences in the shift from a premodern to a modern concept of childhood.

The printing press in Europe produced the first book in 1450. At the beginning of the sixteenth century, European presses had been in production for fifty years, producing

> some 30,000–50,000 different editions . . . [which] have survived, representing 10,000–15,000 different texts. . . . Assuming an average print run to be no greater than 500, then about 20 million books were printed before 1500.[79]

In the early decades of the sixteenth century, then, there must have already existed a large nonclerical reading public. Reading as a skill and as an activity had become marginally public, no longer confined to the university or monastic orders. The availability and consumption of a variety of reading material does not ensure, of course, an immediate change in social values and attitudes, or the wide spread of literacy.

> It is fairly obvious at the outset that printing brought about no sudden or radical transformation, and contemporary culture hardly seems at first to have changed, at least in regards its general characteristics . . . [but] the printed book could be said to have "arrived" between 1500 and 1510.[80]

It was in the early decades of the sixteenth century in Germany that the presses furthered, on a large scale, the ideological aims of a few to sway the opinions of a nation: Luther's Reformation movement.

> [The] state of affairs changed abruptly in 1517 in Germany, a little later and more gradually elsewhere. Religious issues swiftly became questions of the foremost importance and unleashed the strongest passions. For the first time in history there developed a propaganda campaign conducted through the medium of the press. The capacity of the press to serve the interests of those who wished to influence thought and mould public opinion was revealed.[81]

A central component of Luther's prescription for a "truly" Christian way of life was his concern for correct training of the young. And so, a substantial part of Reformation literature, or propaganda as historians Strauss and L. Febvre and H. J. Martin note, became the first and most influential educational treatise of the modern era. With the support of state electorates, princes and dukes, Luther secularized education by institutionalizing compulsory schooling under state control — a revolutionary and historically unprecedented move. In 1896, book printing and literary historian Putnam noted:

> The historians of the time are certainly in substantial accord in the conclusion that the enormous impetus given to the education and active-mindedness of the people through the distribution and the eager acceptance of the writings of the Reformers, the habits then formed of buying and of reading printed books, the incentive secured for the work of the printers and the booksellers, and the practice that came into vogue of circulating books and pamphlets by means of pedlars and colporteurs in districts far beyond the reach of the book-shops, had both an immediate and an abiding effect upon the reading habits of the German people.[82]

In light of the "communications revolution" well under way in the sixteenth century, we might ask to what extent a new mode of communication influenced public opinion, private attitudes and, hence, social support of political decisions? Did mechanized typography influence knowledge relations and discourse formations? Can the "revival of interest in education" be taken as indicative of changing attitudes among adults towards children? Or was this interest in education not a product of the more dominant religious and, indeed, political motivations of reformers such as Luther and the politicians of the ruling aristocracy? Finally, in response to Aries' and this study's concern with changing concepts of childhood, since the beginnings of a shift from the premodern to the modern concept of childhood coincided with the first century of printing, then "why not consider, first of all, how childrearing and schooling were affected by the printed book?"[83] And since the response of church and state to the potential of the presses was not uniform across Europe, it is important to consider the differences between countries that encouraged printers and publishers, and those that opposed or censored the new book-learning.

Printing and Literacy in Catholic France and Protestant Germany

Catholic France strongly resisted the new book trade and issued numerous edicts throughout the early sixteenth century to stem the tide of heretical Protestant literature. By contrast, Protestantism was based on the idea that individuals should have access to scriptures and, hence, to salvation unmediated by clerical intervention. The Council of Trent (1545–1563) prohibited the distribution of vernacular Bibles in all Catholic regions, whereas they were "made almost compulsory for Protestants."[84]

As early as 1515, only two years prior to Luther's posting of the ninety-five theses, Pope Leo X issued an edict to all nations of the Holy Roman Empire, ordering "that no licence should be given for the printing of a book until it had been examined and approved by an authorized representative of the Church."[85] The authority of the church over the production of literature was "contested in Venice, and was never accepted in Germany. In France, on the other hand, the necessity for such ecclesiastical supervision was at once admitted."[86]

The supervisory representative body of the church was the Theological Faculty of the University of Paris and the Paris Parlèment. Parlèment seats were, in Putnam's words, a "kind of circuit court"; members were "officially" appointed by the Crown, but Francis I sold seats to supportive allies. The Parlèment of Paris was not dissolved until 1790. In 1525, a parliamentary edict prohibited the private possession of copies of the Old or New Testament; the edict ordered all copies to be turned in to court notaries. Printers were prohibited from printing any versions of the Testaments under the threat of confiscation of their premises and goods, and banishment from the kingdom.

A 1530 decree "forbade the printing of any work of medical science which had not received the approval of 'three good and notable' doctors of the Faculty of Medicine of the University."[87] That same year, publication of fortune-telling books or almanacs was prohibited under penalty of imprisonment or a fine of ten francs. A 500 franc fine and banishment was the penalty under a 1521 parliamentary decree for printing any polemical or interpretive work of the scriptures unauthorized by the Theological Faculty. This same decree was reissued in 1542, only this time aimed at the booksellers dealing in unauthorized copies.

Despite such discouraging legislation and the apparently successful enforcement of these laws, in major urban centers a black market book trade developed. Those who could afford black market prices, those who could read and were intent on acquiring certain texts could certainly find them in their own country, or just across the borders.[88]

It is not unreasonable to assume that the expansion of a vernacular book-reading public was more restricted in France compared with Protestant regions in Germany where the vernacular German Bible was an essential part of the new faith. Printing centers in Germany expanded rapidly in the years following 1517. The Frankfurt Book Fair was the established center for the European book trade, and as the contemporary statistics indicate, the production of Reformation literature printed in high and low German reflects the arrival and preeminence of the printed vernacular word in early sixteenth century Germany.

> The total number of separate works (principally pamphlets, 'Flugschriften') printed in German in 1513 was 90; in 1518, 146; in 1520, 571; and in 1523, 944. The aggregate for the ten years is 3113. Of the total for the decade, no less than 600 were printed in Wittenberg, a place which before 1517 had not possessed a printing press; this is an indication of the immediate effect produced by the Lutheran movement upon the work of the printers.[89]

Putnam links the output of the presses to a reading public that he assumes to have had basic reading skills:

> It is not so easy at this period to understand how the middle and lower classes in Germany had been able, by the beginning of the sixteenth century, to secure so general a proficiency in reading as to be able to profit by the pamphlet literature of the time, but, that a widespread elementary education existed, is evident from the circulation secured for these pamphlets, and from their immediate influence upon opinion and belief.[90]

Looking to the second century of printing, Eisenstein hypothesizes that printing—engendering new forms of social relations through its "democratizing" effects, as McLuhan saw it—may have had such far-reaching, and not implausible influences as locating the industrial revolution in a particular place and time.

> Given a clearly defined incentive to learn to read was present among Protestants qua Protestants and not among Catholics qua Catholics; for example, one might expect to find a deeper social penetration of literacy among the former than among the latter during the second century of printing. Earlier lines dividing literate from unlettered social strata—magistrates, merchants and masters from journeymen, artisans and yeo-

men — might grow fainter in Protestant regions and more indelible in Catholic ones between the 1550s and 1650s. This, in turn, would affect the timing of 'revolutions of rising expectations' and help to account for different patterns of social agitation and mobility, political cleavage and cohesion. We know that the mechanization of most modes of production came much more gradually in France than in England.[91]

The restricted access in sixteenth century France to vernacular books of popular interest, the Council of Trent having prohibited vernacular theological as well as secular literature, might well explain why historical studies of childhood focused on France identify major change in parental attitude and educational practice to have occurred as late as the seventeenth and eighteenth centuries. The changes brought about by Reformation leaders during the sixteenth century in Germany, in conjunction with the mass utilization of the presses generated rapid and fundamental social and political change in general, and radical educational change in particular. Moreover, "the spread of print between 1450 and 1517, did much to prepare Germany and certain other parts of Europe for the success of Luther's teachings."[92] We might hypothesize, then, that the changing concept of childhood and attendant schooling and childrearing practices was not a universal phenomenon in postmedieval Europe, but that sixteenth century Germany substantially predated France in the shift from a premodern to a modern concept of childhood.

Reformation historian Strauss has also challenged Aries on this point. As noted earlier, Aries' contention is that the extension of childhood, that is, the "creation" of adolescence, did not occur until the eighteenth century. Aries translates this shift to mark the identifiable emergence of a modern concept of childhood, characterizing a pivotal point in European social and intellectual history. Strauss comments on Aries' overgeneralization:

> Aries is wrong in maintaining that it was only in the eighteenth century that the concept of a long childhood was translated into grade schools.[93]
>
> . . . .
>
> *The Journal of Psychohistory*, 1977, (5) 2: 271–90, also challenges the contention of Aries, John R. Gillis, John Demos, and others that the concept of adolescence emerged only as late as the nineteenth century.[94]

Rejecting Aries' claim of a "deliberate humiliation" and "degrading discipline" that "became a feature of the new attitude to childhood,"[95] Strauss notes that:

> Aries refers primarily to France but clearly intends his judgements to apply to Western Europe society as a whole.[96]

Strauss had noted Aries' tendency to generalize from his exclusively French historical data to European history in general. Yet given the aim of *Luther's House of Learning*, Strauss does not develop this problem in Aries' work — and so we find these observations by Strauss confined to reference notes. This study intends to clarify Aries' "judgements" and, in agreement with Strauss' observations, will consider *Centuries of Childhood* as a point of departure.

What follows, then, is a not a refutation of Aries' work, but an examination of the extent to which printing as a communicative technology was a formative feature in the development of a textual and institutional discourse on pedagogical practices and the ideas adults held about childhood. The historical relationship between printing and issues pertaining to childhood will be considered in terms of three historical "fields of emergence": the spread of printing, the secular discourse on childcare and childrearing, and the religious-political discourse on education. In the course of identifying a potential relationship between printing and Reformation ideology, we may come to see how the religious-pedagogical aims of the reformers and the humanistic ideals of the "new pedagogy" were transposed to the discourse on childhood.

3

Typography and Reformation

THIS chapter traces the early development of the printing industry from 1450 to about 1550. Several implications of the new communications technology for the spread of literacy, the rise of Protestantism, and the popularization of the secular and religious discourse on childrearing are discussed. Books—particularly the Bible and popular books of conduct and domestic management—became part of household acquisitions for many families. Of course many peasant and burgher households continued to conduct everyday affairs without reference to book knowledge. Yet print infiltrated homes and communities on calendars, broadsheets heralding upcoming community and regional events, or the many popular almanacs and herbals. Luther's many pamphlet publications—after 1520 less concerned with doctrinal disputes and more focused on moralizing about everyday issues—were written in vernacular high and low German that gave a greater number of people more ready access to both their own language and the ideology Luther was promoting. Print, or "the book" as Febvre and Martin note, had definitely "arrived" by the early 1500s.

The rapid spread of the presses and print information during the first fifty years of printing had a significant impact on literacy, standardizing language and popularizing the vernacular. In all, the printing press paved the way for the standardization and formalization of all discourses—from medicine to homemaking to theology. The possibilities enabled by Gutenberg's invention—a modified winepress—included the emergence of new discourses, the most historically notable being Luther's revolutionary theology: a discourse on individualism. Luther's redefinition of the individual's relationship to God led him to consider closely the nature of childhood. A fundamental component of his vision for a reformed Christian social order was childhood and youth: the nurture of children by the family and the education of children by the school.

Because printing enabled the rapid production of multiple texts, coupled with the possibility of mass distribution of large numbers of the same text, Luther's ideas circulated—materially, in the book or pamphlet—among diverse strata of the German population. The child became a focal object of the early Protestant discourse not only in an ideational context but, importantly, in a material con*text*: print. Whereas childcare had been, for centuries, the domain of women's work and coded in the medium of oral language, at the beginning of the sixteenth century in Germany, men began to take a noticeable interest in children. Pedagogues, moralists, and physicians suddenly became the "new experts" on childcare who published vast numbers of medical health-care books, domestic conduct, and household management guides. All devoted considerable thought to the care and upbringing of children.

Prior to the mass production of printed text throughout the sixteenth century, manuscript text had been available only to a minority of learned men of letters. Commonsense, everyday knowledge—including that concerning the treatment and rearing of children—was coded in the actions, behaviors and spoken language of those who dealt with children: parents, siblings, wetnurses, relatives, and teachers. Print, however, fixed the ideas about children previously encoded in behavior—ways of doing things—into symbolic form which was further affixed to the material object of the book. "Discourse," as Foucault tells us, "was not originally a thing, a product, or a possession, but an action . . . it was a gesture . . . long before it became a possession caught in a circuit of property values."[1]

The materialization of ideas and practices in books, previously transmitted orally and learned by imitation, formalized the (oral) discourse on childhood in the sense that the "subjective," ephemeral word (and action) was replaced by the "authority" of the printed word. The discourse on childhood—which Aries tells us was absent prior to the eighteenth century—had resided in speakers, not books; and speakers do not leave a historical trace. Once "the word" was removed from speakers, however authoritative, the word became objectified in print assuming a new status of objectivity and authority. Freed from subjective authorship of speakers, words and statements—the discourse—took on an apparent objectivity and authority in the medium of print which, according to Foucault, has an expressive function independent of an author.[2]

The emergence of the child on the material surface of the printed page during the first fifty to one hundred years of mechanized typography created an authoritative discourse in which dominant, emergent and residual ideas about children coexisted. The dominant, long-established notions about children were, in large part, residual parts of a discourse on children that had their source in the works of medieval and classical scholars: Quintilian, Saint Jerome, Avicenna, Johann Agricola, Albertus Magnus, and others. The emergent ideas—Luther's revised social and spiritual program—which would, in a few decades, assume a dominant privileged status in a number of discourses, were themselves a reappropriation of Saint Augustine's theology.

The emergent sixteenth century discourse on childhood, then, as it surfaced during the early decades of the Reformation contained within it a resemblance to ideas articulated in the past (e.g., Saint Augustine). This emergent discourse differed from existing discourses about children—the discursive "ground"—since it occupied a new space upon which the initial formation (i.e., new concepts and redefinitions of existing ones) of a whole series of discursive objects and practices was inscribed. What was to be unitized and labelled by historians as "Protestantism" or "Lutheranism" was initially formed on the printed page: the pamphlets, books, and *"Flugschriften."* Even before people were moved to action in either support of or protest against Luther, his (re)formulation of spiritual and civil conduct took shape on the printed page. On the material surface of print and in the ideational domains of religious, political and sociocultural discourses, historically new statements emerged (e.g., individualism) linked, in some instances, to historically established and authoritative ones (e.g., seven-year developmental stages of "man"; the doctrine of innate sin). The discourse on childhood emerged as part of a series of separate but related discourses on individualism, secularism, nationalism, matrimony, the family, the state, and so forth. What we might call Luther's "social theory," grounded in religious doctrine, touched on almost all aspects of civil and spiritual life in efforts to redefine and redirect the social, political an religious affairs of a nation.

As Foucault points out, a formalized discourse is legitimate knowledge in the sense that it is always in a unity (*"oeuvre"*) and always encoded in an authoritative medium of expression: the book, the manuscript or embodied in the cleric or tribal elder. It is these unities that the historian must dispense with in order to uncover the underlying discursive relations and divisions they engender. We can analyze the textual historical trace freed from its totalizing labels (periodization, authorship), but we cannot analyze the formalized discourse that was manifest only in speech and action. We are confined, then, to undertake an historical discursive analysis constrained by the presence (and corresponding absence) of a material record — material in the sense that textual statements are objects of perception and are spatio-temporally present.

Discourse — "residual materiality" — is encoded in forms of recording: a list, a book, a map, journals, diaries, or architecture and so forth. These texts have meaning (for a current reading) even if they are apprehended as autonomous and independent of author and historical *"oeuvre"* because texts have interpretive and expressive functions that "outlive" authors and previous readers. D'Amico explains:

> The residual materiality then is not the meaning of those statements as that is understood by some particular reader. Rather, meaning is possible because, in a manner of speaking, these bodies of discourse outlive any specific reader or author and replicate again and again a more abstract structure independent of their spatio-temporal origins and, . . . their author's intended effects (if they even have an individual author).[3]

Much as the texts of history give us access to the discourse of history, the texts available to readers contemporaneous with the historical text incorporated those readers into a given discourse. Simply put: the sixteenth century household guides constituted the prescriptive code for ways of doing things and the reader consuming the text entered into a relationship with the text positing her or him into the field of discursive practice. Whether the reader acted upon the prescriptions in the text or not, in significant or marginal ways, is immaterial. The uptake of what was in the text need not be transformed into verifiable social action at the level of the event (e.g., the end of swaddling; the beginning of mass literacy; the practice of child abandonment). The text in its material presence became itself a part of discursive practice by being materially present in the social sphere of the household. Moreover, once the reader had enunciated the text's ideational content (regardless of individual difference of interpretation), the discourse "circulated" in the sphere of everyday practice: perhaps only in the mind of the reader, perhaps surfacing in everyday action in imperceptible ways.

We can nonetheless hypothesize that once (some) parents read, say, the physician Rösslin's popular book about childcare, that perhaps some aspects of childcare underwent modification. Or, certain taken-for-granted assumptions about, for instance, infant's insensitivity to "coarse woollen cloth or scratchy swaddling bands"[4] may have encouraged some parents to reconsider their perceptions of infants' sensitivity to physical discomfort which may, in turn, have led parents to change the ways in which they bedded their children. Or, consider Luther's call to all parents to send their children to school in his popular pamphlet, *A Sermon on Keeping Children in School*, that served polemical and practical purposes; many parents did comply with Luther's request by sending their children to existing and new public schools. But also, many parents did in fact refuse to send their children to school despite Luther's appeals, as he was to find out on one of the first major school visitations. The discursive statements in this instance circulated in the minds of the readers (of, say, the *Sermon*) and perhaps surfaced in conversations and discussions among families, between neighbors and within communities. Refusal to send children to school can, however, also be seen as resistance — and therefore discursive practice — contra the discursive imperative: send and keep the children in school.

On another level of textual authority, the increased presence of printed material in the homes of an increasing cross-section of the sixteenth century Protestant population, can be seen to have changed the status of print from one previously considered as the property of an elite (professionals, clerics, academics), to print in the vernacular accessible to private ownership by all social classes. Wider text accessibility — both cognitively and financially — would give the text credibility as a source of information that the common burgher previously did not have access to.

And as more and more printed text in the vernacular and on topics of everyday concern dispersed among the populace, so did the ideas that readers took from text spread into public (institutional) and private (family) life. On these "uninscribed spaces" discursive practices would form: ways of doing and thinking about certain things. Initially, such formation of practices were undoubtedly irregular and inconsistent among different sites, different communities, among and within families. But, over the decades, as text became increasingly standardized, plentiful, and as text itself became institutionalized (i.e., in the school), discursive practices focused on the child's body and mind and became more regular (and regulated) in tandem with the standardization of the text—the formal discourse—for and about children.

In this chapter, then, we will consider the relationships among the emergent communications technology of typography, the spread and the kind of print information that the presses produced, the diffusion of pro-Lutheran presses and Luther's early pamphlet evangelism. Luther's calculated use of the press has not gone unnoticed by historical observers. And it is the possibility of mass production and mass distribution afforded by the printing press that enabled Luther to mass promote his revolutionary ideas so rapidly and so widely. This chapter concludes by situating those pivotal years of the 1520s—the years after the posting of the ninety-five theses in 1517 and the years prior to the 1525 Peasant Rebellion—in the context of northern Europe's economic and sociopolitical conditions. It is not implausible that Europe's economic and political crises, particularly in Germany, set the conditions of possibility—threshold conditions—that constrained and precipitated what was to be known as Protestantism to emerge in the forms and places that it did.

The Spread of Printing: 1450–1500

Johannes Gensfleisch zum Gutenberg invented the printing press in Mainz, Germany sometime between 1448 and 1451. As early as 1437, in a suit filed against Gutenberg in Strassburg, the words "press" and "printing" appear in a legal document.[5] The first printed book, a Latin Bible, was printed by Gutenberg's press between 1452 and 1455; the first edition of the first book was produced in 200 copies.[6] Two years later, in 1457, Füst and Schöffer, Gutenberg's troublesome business partners, produced a Latin Psalter, "a book of superlative accomplishments." That same year, a *Mainz Kalender* was printed. This first printed "medical" text was a "bleeding and purgation calendar, which gave details of the lucky and unlucky days on which to bleed or take medicine in a given year."[7]

At the University of Cologne, a press was installed and the first book produced in 1466. "At the end of the century, there were more than 20 printers in the city [Cologne]."[8] In 1479, the first Bible in Dutch was printed at Cologne. Lübeck, north of Hamburg, was the first center in the north to install a press in 1473. The first German Bible was produced by a Strassburg printer, Johann Mentelin, whose profession was a "writer in gold or illustrator of manuscripts."[9]

A Mainz printer, Berthold Ruppel, who had worked with Gutenberg, moved to Basel and established the first printing shop there in 1467. Johann Amerbach, widely considered a truly "Renaissance" artist, was introduced to the "art of printing" by one of his teachers in Paris who had first introduced printing to that city. Amerbach, after completing a Master of Arts at the University of Paris, eventually worked as a corrector in a printing shop in Nüremberg. He later settled in Basel where he set up a printing shop that was to become the center of intellectual activity, superseded later by the House of Froben, friend and publisher of Erasmus. Johann Reuchlin's work was published by Amerbach, and Sebastian Brant's *Narrenschiff* (Ship of Fools) was published there in 1494.[10] In Augsburg, the first book came off the presses in 1468, the year of Gutenberg's death.

In Nüremberg, however, the largest printing works in Germany were established by Anton Koberger:

> more than a hundred people worked on 24 presses . . . [Koberger] dealt in books for other printers, and it may be assumed that he also had a bookbinding works operating on his behalf.[11]

In the field of graphic arts, the Koberger shop was preeminent: among the artists who worked for him were Dürer's teachers and, later, Dürer as well.

In Italy, Venice was the center of printing. Johann Numeister, a pupil of Gutenberg, established a print shop in Foligno, returned to Mainz, and then moved to France where he opened yet another printing business at Lyons. Another Italian printer, the humanist lecturer Aldus Manutius, produced his first book, a Greek grammar in 1494. A few years later he

> created a revolutionary innovation in printing in that he printed books of small format in an italic type; this type was said to be an imitation of Petrarch's handwriting.[12]

In 1470, two professors at the Sorbonne invited three German printers to set up a press at the university and teach the art of printing. Independent presses had already been in operation in France since the late 1450s; by the 1470s the first university press was established in Paris. An English merchant, William Caxton had acquired the skills of printing at Cologne in the 1460s; during the early 1470s he operated a press in Bruges and in 1476 he left for England to establish the first press at Westminster.[13]

The 'German art' was established in Budapest in the year 1473, in London in 1477, in Oxford in 1478, in Denmark in 1482, in Stockholm in 1483, in Moravia in 1486, and in Constantinople in 1490.[14]

In the last year of the fifteenth century, the first woodcut depicting a printing press appeared in an edition of the *Dance of Death*, printed at Lyons in February, 1499.[15] It is an eerie woodcut, foreshadowing public book burnings, book censorship laws, and later claims by reactionary theologians that books were the works of the devil.

Before 1500, about 45,000 books had been printed by presses set up in 206 European cities.[16] Febvre and Martin estimate that by 1500, 35,000 editions had been produced in fifteen to twenty million copies printed in 236 western European towns.[17] During the first fifty years of printing, the reading audience was confined to "men of letters": clerics, university professors, the educated nobility, and the printers themselves; "thus university cities, monasteries, the church and princely residences were the main purchasers."[18]

As books were mostly unbound and sold as collections of printed sheets, bookbinding was "left to the taste of the individual,"[19] and was not part of the book production process. Title pages were not utilized until the turn of the century, and author, title, date, printer and place of printing were inconsistently recorded. Printers between 1450 and 1500 were specialists in all aspects of book printing: typecasting, typesetting, proof reading, ink mixing, the mechanics of printing, collating, designing ornamental rubrics and the large illuminated letters that prefaced the first word of each page. The early sixteenth century saw an increasing specialization of labor in the production of books. The art of printing was well established, having become a commercially viable business by the end of the fifteenth century. Increasing demand for books led to expansion of the printing shop in terms of acquiring more presses and hiring more specialized help: craftsmen to design and carve the woodblocks, metal workers to cast the type, and bookbinders. Latin predominated in most editions still primarily aimed at the learned elite who had the benefit of institutional financial support for the acquisition of, at the time, relatively expensive books.

The first fifty years of printing produced primarily theological works and reproductions of classical texts; the style and format of books replicated the manuscript. During the early decades of the sixteenth century, European printing diversified both in content and format: title pages appeared more frequently with more exacting reference to author, date and publishing firm; the use of more intricately designed woodblocks for illustrations increased; the use of boldface and headpieces became more common; herbals, almanacs, calendars, medical manuals and books, maps, travelogues, and historical chronicles appeared on the book market. Increasingly diverse knowledges were being formalized in book form.

The most elaborate and aesthetically impressive history text, the *Nüremberg Chronicle*, was produced by Koberger's press in Nüremberg just before the turn of the century in 1493. N. Levarie gives a short account of this "book of monumental ambition":

> The text itself ventured nothing less than a total world history. The illustrating scheme was immensely complex, embracing large double-page topographical cuts of cities which break across the pages in a variety of formations, and figures scattered in and among the text in every imaginable way, sometimes connected by richly coiling vines: over eighteen hundred pictures in all.[20]

During the first half of the sixteenth century, German and Swiss printing centers led Europe in productivity, quality, and diversity of illustrated and scholarly books. The innovative works of Dürer superseded the quality and originality of all other illustrators of his day; his affiliation with Koberger's press in Nüremberg lent additional prestige and income to Nüremberg as a leading cultural and printing center, and enhanced the status of the Koberger works. The prestige of both Dürer and Koberger's enterprise was greatly facilitated by the ambitious Emperor Maximilian I who commissioned not only major architectural projects for the Hapsburg regime, but supported the arts as well. Levarie comments:

> A good number of the Nüremberg and Augsburg artists worked at some time on the many book projects of the Emporer Maximilian . . . some of these projects were so am-

bitious that they were never completed. The *Weisskünig*, which undertook to describe the parentage, education, and exploits of Maximilian with 249 illustrations by Burgmair, was put on a press for the first time two and a half centuries later, in 1775 . . . Dürer himself participated . . . in the most outrageously grand of Maximilian's printing schemes: the *Triumphal Arch and Procession* . . . the Triumphal Arch alone consisted of 192 woodcuts which combined covered an area of about ten by twelve feet.[21]

Imperial patronage of the arts and financial support coupled with the already established prestige of the Koberger presses, placed Nüremberg at the center of the printing industry, attracting members of learned circles, literate laymen, clergy, artists, and aristocratic patrons of the arts.[22] Nüremberg's cultural status was rivalled only by Basel and Strassburg. Mainz at the end of the fifteenth century had lost its lead and importance as a major center of printing.[23]

The book had come of age by 1500. The increasing output of books in vernacular high and low German undoubtedly gave more people access to information traditionally written in Latin. And although Latin still predominated in scholarly works,

> Latin began to lose ground during the 16th century. From 1530 onwards, this process becomes unmistakable . . . the bookreading public became from then on . . . increasingly a lay public—made up in large part of women and of merchants, many of whom had hardly any knowledge of Latin.[24]

One would assume that scholarly works in geography and the natural sciences were of less interest to the general public. Yet these more "disciplinary works"—anatomy, botany, zoology, and geography texts—were plentiful and, unlike most devotional works, were accompanied by intricate engravings and woodblock prints. According to Febvre and Martin, the visual appeal of these books made them a popular item among more "enlightened amateurs":

> Such sumptuous productions with their magnificent wood blocks found a ready public of enlightened amateurs who were probably often attracted to particular volumes by other than purely scientific reasons.[25]

A growing public interest in the world outside the community and country can be inferred from the number of re-editions and translations many of these books underwent. And as the works in geography broadened the readers' worldview outward, so to speak, the equally popular medical books focused the readers' attention inward. In perhaps imperceptible ways, one can assume the worldviews, the assumptions and range of ideas of the reading public to have changed subtly. And as the more specialized works of anatomy, surgery, or geography became available in German, the spoken language was slowly transformed into a legitimate medium of expression for formal discourse—in literature, medicine, pedagogy, and religion. Ideas were more systematically encoded through increasing standardization of grammar, vocabulary, and orthography.

The systemization of ideas in more uniform linguistic categories and the materialization of those ordered ideas in books, helped to unify and fix sets of ideas within a given discourse.[26] Furthermore, the mass distribution of standardized ideas systematized discourse by dispersing a material unit of ideas (i.e., a book or pamphlet) among a variety of readers, thus unifying them linguistically and, to a certain extent, in shared cultural knowledge. Febvre and Martin note that,

> the standardization of grammar and vocabulary is even more important than spelling in establishing a language that can be readily understood by one and all . . . [and] by encouraging the multiplication of the number of texts available in the vernacular the printing press everywhere favored . . . the development and the systemization of the literary language of the nation.[27]

As the vernaculars established themselves as formal literary and scholarly languages, a sense of political and cultural unity developed more strongly. And as the linguistic and theological corpus was normed and standardized, people came to recognize that their language, indeed, had an official and national status. This emerging sense of nationalism was particularly important for those member states of the German Empire that had harbored resentment of their political, religious and cultural annexation to the Holy Roman Empire for too long. Chaytor explains:

> The invention of printing stabilized the predominant mode of speech, secured its position as the official and literary

medium, and thereby reduced dialects. . . . The next step is to regard the official language as a national heritage and an expression of national character. This idea made slow progress so long as the wars of religion continued . . . but the growth of literature and the spread of education consequent upon the greater multiplication of books increased its strength continually.[28]

And while printing encouraged a sense of internal, national unity, printed translations encouraged an international exchange of indigenous literary works. By the early 1500s, although religious themes still dominated the book market, the printing of secular literature steadily increased. In addition to vernacular prayer and song books, popular works for everyday domestic use such as herbals, household manuals, and family conduct guides reached increasingly diverse audiences.

Books of Conduct for Family and Children

Albrecht von Eyb, born in Germany (c. 1420) and educated in Bologna and Padua, was a prolific writer strongly influenced by the Italian humanist movement of the late fifteenth century. Two of his most popular works were reprinted by the Koberger press in Nüremberg as late as 1520, fifty-five years after von Eyb's death. The *Ehebuch* (Book of Marriage) was written in German and, broadly, discusses the virtues of marriage or remaining single. The Latin *Margarita Poetica* (variously interpreted as *Pearl of Poetry* or *Pearl of Humanism*), was "a handbook of rhetoric and letter writing . . . the first substantial book of this type composed by a German author."[29] How-to manuals for reading and writing were to become increasingly popular throughout the century.

Caspar Huberinus, a Lutheran and popular author, wrote the most influential and widely read family conduct books. *Spiegel der Hauszucht* (The Household Mirror), published in Nüremberg in 1552, "condemns tyrannical husbands and evil wives."[30] Huberinus' other widely read work was *Der kleine Catechismus für die Jugend zu gebrauchen* (A Shorter Catechism for the Instruction of Young People), published in Augsburg in 1544.[31]

Jörg Wickram's *Good and Bad Neighbors* (1556) is a treatise on the community of Christian households. "He wished to show how pious families can live together in peace and friendship. He tried to demonstrate that hard work in one's appointed calling leads to public esteem and inner contentment."[32] Repeatedly, family conduct books stressed the importance of normalizing family relations. Women, no longer consigned to nunneries since girlhood and no longer forced into prearranged marriage, prostitution or spinsterhood, were to take up God's work in the holy estate of matrimony as loving and faithful wives and mothers. Men, likewise, liberated from "false chastity" and a corrupt life in monasteries, were to take their place in marriage as equally loving and faithful husbands and fathers. "Popular literature lampooned both wastrel husbands and faithless wives, both wife-beaters and shrews."[33] Intrafamilial discord was seen by humanists and theologians alike as the central negative catalyst of greater social disintegration, reflected in church, state, and community disharmony. A cohesive family unit was considered an imperative precondition for a stable and cohesive society.

In Wickram's *Good and Bad Neighbors* we also note that hard work in an appointed calling, rewarded by inner contentment, mirrors an existential and spiritual ethic that prompted Max Weber three and a half centuries later to reevaluate the relationship between the "religious characteristics . . . of the old Protestant spirit and modern capitalism."[34] Among Wickram's many other works, one is specifically concerned with young boys' conduct: *Der Jungen Knaben Spiegel* (The Young Boys' Mirror), published in 1554.[35]

In 1536, a Wittenberg press published Johann Böhm's *Ein Christliches Radtbüchlein für die Kinder* (A Christian Advice Booklet for Children). Johann Agricola wrote *Eine Christliche Kinderzucht inn Gottes Wort und Lere: Aus der Schule zu Eisleben* (A Christian Child Training Manual in God's Words and Teaching: From the School at Eisleben), which was published in Wittenberg in 1527.[36] The following year, in 1528, Luther commissioned Agricola to write a catechism. This request by Luther may have been on the basis of Agricola's 1527 publication: the catechism, published in 1528 in Wittenberg was entitled *Hundert und dreissig Gemeyner Fragestücke für die jungen Kinder ynn der deudschen Meydin Schule zu Eyssleben.* This work was oriented towards more pedagogical ends as the title indicates: "130 Questions for Young Children in the German Meydin School at Eisleben"; Luther had been a student at Eisleben as a child.

Veit Dietrich wrote *Kinder-Postilla* (Children's Postulates), which was published at Nüremberg in 1549. Another marriage conduct manual, *Ehespiegel* (Marriage Mirror) was written by Cyriacus Spangenberg in 1563 and printed in Strassburg. A bedtime prayer-book for children, *Bettbüchlein* (Bedbooklet) was written by Andreas

Musculus and published in Leipzig. Erasmus Alberus wrote a series of ten essays for parents providing instructions to aid young children learning to speak: *Zehen Dialogi für Kinder, so anfangen zu reden,* (Ten Dialogues for Children who are Learning to Speak) published in Nüremberg.[37]

Felix Würtz, a barber-surgeon, wrote extensively on the health care of women and children. His best known work, *Practica der Wund-Artzney* (A Practical Manual of Medical Care), published in 1563, has a short work for children appended to it. From the title of the appended work, *Schönes und nützliches Kinder-Büchlein* (A Pretty and Useful Children's Booklet), it is not clear whether this booklet was a story or health guide written for children, or whether it was intended as a parental guide to children's ailments. Strauss suggests that Würtz was "a widely trusted medical adviser . . . [judging] from the circulation of his books in several languages."[38] Würtz showed great sympathy and compassion for children. Würtz condemned the use of standing stools for small children which inhibited their mobility and forced them to stand upright for long periods. His criticism of these stools suggests their common use and indicates concern for children's comfort. Würtz writes:

> There are stools for children to stand in, in which they can turn around in any way, when mothers or nurses see them in it, then they care no more for the child, let it alone, go about their own business, supposing the child to be well provided, but they little think on the pain and misery the poor child is in . . . the poor child . . . must stand maybe many hours, whereas half an hour standing is too long . . . I wish that all such standing stools were burned.[39]

The absence of consistent reference to the scriptures as justification for certain childraising practices or the curing of disease, make Würtz's work appear uncharacteristic of his age. He strongly rejected swaddling and the use of wetnurses, a practice in vogue among the nobility. Strauss quotes Würtz's sympathies for the newborn:

> Imagine what goes on in him as he feels the touch of rough hands on his tender skin and is chafed by coarse woollen cloth or scratchy swaddling bands. What do you think it feels like to lie on a hard board covered with prickly straw, sharp-edged planing chips, or crumbled birch leaves?[40]

Clearly concerned here with the potential consequences of infants' perception of physical discomfort, Würtz also gives us an indication of what may have been prevalent practices and conditions awaiting the newborn. As Strauss observes:

> States of insecurity induced by discomfort, injury, or excessive restraint recur in nightmares, Würtz thinks. If they persist they will leave the child with a permanently melancholy disposition.[41]

Würtz's denouncement of infant care practices may suggest that parental lack of concern for children's physical comfort was common — common enough for Würtz to advise against swaddling, standing-stools and uncomfortable bedding. In this particular instance, adult disregard for children's comfort and psychological security, as Würtz saw it, could be taken to lend credence to Aries' claim of parental indifference towards the young. But indifference should not be confused with ignorance. If "prickly straw," "crumbled birch leaves," or "coarse woollen cloth" was all that was available to most parents with which to bed their children, we cannot accuse them of neglect; nor can we accuse them of indifference for not forming educated hypotheses, as Würtz did, of what possible psychological effects rough bedding, standing stools, or swaddling might have on young children. Yet, if Würtz's observations of child care practices can be interpreted as indicative of widespread parental indifference to children, then his prescriptions for more parental sensitivity for infants' physical and psychological needs can be taken to signify affective concern with the welfare of children predating Stone's eighteenth century and Aries' seventeenth century shift in parental attitude towards the young. Contrary to Aries' claims of a benign indifference towards childhood in the premodern era which, beginning in the sixteenth century, was transformed into a reign of terror over the young, Würtz's work and that of other pediatricians and pedagogues testifies to (male) concern about and sensitivity towards children, including newborn infants.

The fact that men did write a great deal about infants' probable perceptions of parental treatment gives the impression that the upbringing of children — not only their mere survival but also their physical comfort, psychological security, social adjustment, and their education — was very much a popular, as well as academic concern. Not only does the substantial volume of literature about children addressed to parents discount both Aries' and Stone's premise of parental indifference, neglect and brutality, but the intricate detail in which childbearing and childrearing was discussed as well as the consistent admonitions to parents to treat the young kindly and with affection is itself a positive comment on sixteenth century attitudes towards infancy and childhood.

Pediatric Literature

While much of our knowledge about the impact of print on ideas about children must be drawn from inferences, some specific evidence, such as the early pediatric manuals, remains. The advice for childrearing offered parents in domestic guides and pediatric manuals provides a fairly well-defined concept of childhood and of childrearing practices.

In G.F. Still's *History of Pediatrics*, we find a reproduction of the earliest printed poem on the care of children, *Versehung des Leibs* (Care of the Body), written in Swabian by Heinrich von Louffenburg in 1429 and printed in Augsburg in 1491. A part of this poem was translated into high German and titled *Ein Regiment der Gesundheit Für die jungen Kinder* (A Regimen of Health for Young Children), published in 1532 and reedited in 1544. Still summarizes Louffenburg's pediatrics:

> The pediatric part of Louffenburg's poem included in this book begins with directions as to the regimen of the pregnant woman, and then deals with the following points: how to manage new-born children; how to bathe them and how to look after them asleep and awake; how to feed and suckle them; how to manage them when the teeth begin to appear; how the wet-nurse is to be suitable; how long children should be suckled and how to wean them from the milk.[42]

Four woodcuts are included in the four pages of the 1549 edition reproduced in Still's book. They confirm the practice of swaddling but also, surprisingly, illustrate rather advanced, modern childrearing devices and methods. On the instruction for the care of pregnant women the woodcut shows a woman holding a swaddled infant; she sits, looking down at the child, next to a table on which a small bowl and small spoon are placed — the illustration exudes a warm simplicity. The small bowl and spoon indicate that the transition from breast milk to solid foods occurred some time around ten or twelve months while infants were still swaddled.

The woodcut in the section discussing the proper care and placement of infants in cradles shows a woman rocking a cradle in which a swaddled infant is wrapped into the cradle; the infant's head is propped up on a pillow and the advice for mothers is: "The head must be covered and protected from drafts, the head should also be raised above the prostrate body." A few lines further, sound and timeless advice advocates "singing sweet songs to the infants with a gentle voice to cheer them up and prepare them for a sweet sleep."[43]

The third woodcut is accompanied by a set of rhymed instructions on the problems of teething and learning to walk. Here we see a toddler learning to walk by sitting on a wooden three-wheeled version of our modern tricycle. The child, whose features admittedly resemble "a miniature adult," appears to have trouble remaining balanced on the wheeled walker and looks to the mother in distress; she haltingly leans toward the child with hands outstretched—her posture implies more of a cautioning and guiding reassurance to the child's struggle with the walker, than a reproachful or reprimanding corrective action.

The final woodcut in this series shows the transition from bottle feeding to solid foods. Louffenburg's advice is that after a two year suckling period, mothers must wean the infant, but not too suddenly or too rapidly. Rösslin, the Dr. Spock of sixteenth and seventeenth century Europe, similarly advised against abrupt weaning in his famous prenatal and child care manual *Rosegarten*. The introduction to solid foods requires careful and thoughtful preparation: foods should be sweetened and mashed. Failure to puree and sweeten the infants' broth will most likely result in "stones," cramps in hands, feet and legs. The woodcut shows a woman seated at a table, stirring food in a bowl and looking down at a child seated on a stool next to her and sucking from a baby bottle. The child appears less as a miniature adult, having pudgy limbs and a reasonable resemblance to child-like facial features.

From Louffenburg's *Care of the Body*, we can deduce that child health care was a legitimate concern. Moreover, a gentle and nurturing attitude towards infants was stressed as an important and critical part of children's health care. That infants "did not count," as Aries proposes, is questionable when we read that infants were, indeed, perceived as physically and psychologically vulnerable, in need of specialized attending, and that, contrary to many suggestions, not all children were strapped to boards and hung on wall pegs—many

67

youngsters probably had the privilege of learning to walk in wheeled walkers. Of further interest is the women's attire in the woodcuts; it is not the dress of the well-to-do, but typifies peasant and lower-class city burgher dress; in other words, the *Care of the Body* was addressed to the households of a literate common folk. Moreover, the problems of weaning, teething, or learning to walk were not the concerns of women of the nobility who relegated childrearing to wetnurses. It is also worth noting that the recommended and perhaps commonly accepted practice of weaning at age two is a marked contrast to the general assumption that lower class women breastfed their children long past infancy.

The most famous and most comprehensive work on pediatrics, *Rosegarten*, of which the last known edition was published as late as 1730, was written by a German, Eucharius Rösslin in 1512 and was immediately reissued in 1513.[44] Ozment, writing extensively on Rösslin's contribution to sixteenth century child care, refers to a 1910 reprint of the *Rosegarten* in which it is titled *Rosengarten*.[45] Rösslin was a practicing doctor first at Worms and later at Frankfurt. The first publication was in German and it was subsequently translated into Latin, French, Dutch, and English. Rösslin also wrote a herbal, *Kreuterbuch*, dated 1533. Still notes that the *Rosegarten* "has a special interest as being the first book dealing with this subject [children's diseases and cures] translated into and printed in the English language."[46] It is the first book on pediatrics to have appeared in England, translated by Richard Jonas and published in London in 1540.

Rösslin's *Rosegarten* "was one of the most famous works on midwifery of the period."[47] Included are sections "on the management and feeding of infants and on diseases of children." Various parts of the original German edition of the *Rosegarten* were separately published and appeared as distinct works under various titles including *The Medicine Book of Wedlock, Emergencies of Pregnancy, Child Nurture,* and *Medicine of Women.* We can assume that reprints of sections of the entire *Rosegarten* enabled more people to gain access to the information and, as well, abbreviated versions of the rather voluminous text enabled the reader to purchase a cheaper booklet on a specialized topic.

Another widely circulated and popular vernacular pediatric work was written by physician and humanist Otto Brunfels in the 1530s: *Weiber und Kinder Apothek* (Women and Children's Apothecary). Brunfels, a physician, was also a Strassburg school teacher. A year after taking up his teaching post at the Carmelite Cloister in Strassburg he published a German version of his popular childrearing guide, *On Disciplining and Instructing Children* (1525), which he originally wrote in Latin in 1519.

A *Haus-Apothek* (House Apothecary) by Hieronymus Braunschweig is dated 1537. There seems to be some controversy over authorship between pediatrician Metlinger's version of *A Regimen for Young Children* and Brunfels' *Apothecary*; Still claims that "Brunfels in fact was an unblushing plagiarist,"[48] Brunfels' last chapter is borrowed from Metlinger, entitled *Wie man die Kinde halten und ziehen soll so sy gon und reden lernent biss sy das alter sieben iar erlangent*, or "How to keep and raise children until they learn to speak and until they have reached their seventh year". Age seven marked the end of early childhood; seven year developmental cycles were a popular and traditional explanatory scheme for categorizing the "ages of man." Foucault's notion of "grids of specification" suggests that discourse acts upon an object of study by specifying how, for instance, mind or body is "divided, contrasted, related, regrouped, classified." Seven year developmental cycles here mark such a discursive grid of specification whereby social, physical, and cognitive development is differentiated and classified.

Interest in pediatrics was a part of the revival of interest in medicine during the late fifteenth and early sixteenth century. The medical tracts of antiquity were translated by medical-humanist scholars with the same fervor of the "new learning" that encouraged the translation of standard Greek and Latin philosophical works. Moreover, printing enabled medical scholars to become authors writing from practical experience, addressing the public in their own language. As Strauss notes,

> a surge of interest in pediatrics marked the 16th century when . . . scholarship and printing brought to this branch of medicine a kind of international collaboration. More important . . . the growing respectability of vernacular language freed practicing doctors from their profession's subservience to its classical and Arabic predecessors.[49]

The medical-humanist scholars of the day, many of whom were also practicing physicians, combined traditional knowledge derived from medieval and classical scholarship — Albertus Magnus, Avicenna, Galen, Hippocrates — with the teachings of Rudolf Agricola, "father" of German humanism.

As more vernacular domestic guides and booklets about child health care were being published, we can assume that certain child-rearing practices and ideas about the nature of childhood came to be more widely circulated throughout society. The early pediatric books provided parents with a noninstitutional pedagogy for training the young at home. These works reflect a concept of childhood that valued and stressed parental attention to and affection for children. And devotion to the young, including a father's assitance in infant care, would not go unnoticed by the Holy Father, as Luther noted:

> When a father washes diapers or performs some other mean task for his child, and someone ridicules him as an effeminate fool . . . God with all his angels and creatures is similing.[50]

The Diffusion of Luther's Ideas

In oral cultures, the transmission of information is by word of mouth. In the sixteenth century printed pamphlets were becoming a popular and effective medium for transmitting the reformers' messages to the people. Yet, newsworthy events, political proclamations, or the call to arms continued to be heralded by town criers. Outlying villages tended to be the last and least informed:

> Lutheran gatherings and sermons in towns located along the main roads always drew a better attendance, thanks to the merchants, academicians, master builders, journeymen, beggars, and entertainers. However, in most cases, a direct connection between trade routes and the dispersion of the new faith is hard to establish.[51]

In the early stages of the Reformation, Luther and his followers preached the new approach to the word of God to the common folk by the traditional channel of communication—the sermon. Itinerant pro-Lutheran preachers instructed the rural peasantry in German which more readily made accessible not only the words of the gospel, but enabled the preachers to explain those doctrinal issues in question—communion, mass, indulgences—of which the common peasantry, according to Hannemann, had limited understanding. Hanneman notes that these

> clandestine and itinerant preachers were mostly non-residents in their sphere of influence and used a pseudonym so they

could operate in secrecy and appear as equal in the socioeconomic view of the common people. This made them more
popular among the common folk.[52]

Appearing as "one" with the people, speaking their language, and addressing local concerns, these preachers attracted peasants from
neighboring villages and towns of the region who attended the sermons in increasing numbers and readily converted to the ideas of the
new faith.

The Lutheran evangelists, preaching at clandestine meetings or
preaching officially under local municipal sanction were, nonetheless,
often the target of harassment by local authorities who were either
devout Catholics or ambivalent about the evangelists' activities. Sermons left impressions of ideas in the minds of townfolk, ideas that
were open to misrepresentation and misunderstanding by the very
transitory nature of the spoken word. Had Luther and his followers
been confined to rely only on sermons, personal appearances and
public lectures in their quest to win the support of the German people
against the Church of Rome, we can speculate that the development
and rapid spread of the Reformation may have taken a far more circuitous, if not altogether different route.

The early development of Luther's theology in the 1520s coincided
with the period in which printing was superseding the manuscript
tradition, and book learning had become commonly accepted and
relatively widespread practice among scholars and educated urban
citizens. The traditional methods of oral communication through sermons, public preaching and town criers, coupled with the mass
distribution of and accessibility to printed works, provided the means
for rapid and radical change.

The sixteenth century, then, unlike previous or subsequent centuries marked a transition period from oral/manuscript to print/book
culture. But this transition should not be interpreted as print displac-
ing oral transmission, or the power of the printed word gaining
primacy over the spoken word. Strauss notes that the two cultures,
oral and print, "interpenetrated so deeply and at so many points that
neither could have flourished independently."[53] Reformation historian Cole suggests that "the combination of oral methods with printed
materials as sources of information created a new 'cultural mix' that
was essentially a new force in the sixteenth century."[54] We might argue
that oral practices were, in fact, remade through the advent of print
discourse. Printing did create a cultural mix in terms of making international scholarship and readership possible. For the mass of lower
and middle class burghers, however, the "combination of oral methods

with printed materials" may not necessarily have created a cultural mix. Consider, for instance, that everyday verbal interaction within a community would most likely concern local affairs, and if "print information" was the topic of discussion it would most likely have been derived from local posters, pamphlet literature or the Bible, rather than concern esoteric foreign or scientific works. The rise of indigenous literature during the sixteenth century, seen by historians to have reflected and reinforced a growing sense of nationalism, suggests an emergent class-based cultural insularity, and less of a "cultural mix."[55]

Presses in Support of Luther

The Reformation "involved the great turning point for printing."

> It was now to be shown that the flood of printed works could influence people in a way previously not conceived of. Such a rapid spreading of the doctrines of Luther would have been inconceivable without printing.[56]

In *Die hochdeutschen Drucker der Reformationszeit* or "The High German Printers of the Reformation Period," book historian Götze lists all pro-Lutheran presses from the 1520s to the late 1540s. He cites detailed autobiographical accounts of the printers and lists words specific to given regional dialects which appear in the printed works of local printing shops. Lacking in Götze's list of German printing establishments are the centers in North Germany. He lists a total of eighty-seven printing shops and ten single ownerships of two businesses in separate towns. Febvre and Martin supplement Götze's findings by noting that 140 German towns operated presses throughout the sixteenth century. If 140 towns had printing establishments in the course of the entire century, then Götze's findings of eighty-seven pro-Lutheran printing presses in operation during the thirty years between 1520 and the late 1540s indicates a proportionately large number of presses in the service of the Protestant cause.

The remainder of Götze's book is a compilation of correspondence between printers. These letters indicate not only a genuine cooperation among printers in sharing technical information, but reflect a shared concern with attempts to improve lexical clarity, legibility, quality of print and illustrations. Above all, the letters reflect a new and sophisticated technical terminology. On the "eve of the Reformation," printing was developing both as a lucrative commercial enterprise and in technical sophistication. Mentelin expanded into the paper trade; bookbinding was incorporated as part of the printing process. In Basel, the prestigious printing house of Frobel, Erasmus' publisher, bought a type foundry in 1536.[57]

Wittenberg University was established in 1502. In 1508 Johann Rhau-Grünenberg set up the first press there and "in 1516 he published Luther's earliest works and almost certainly the famous theses on Indulgences on 1517."[58] In 1519, a Leipzig printer, Melchior Lotther, opened a branch plant at Wittenberg that was to become the press entirely in the service of Luther.[59]

In terms of the geography and quality of printing in the 1520s, Febvre and Martin note the development of two important trends subsequent to Luther's rise to prominence. First, the importance of printing in the south declined as north German cities superseded the south in sheer quantity of production. Second, the production of books with traditional "disciplinary" content disappeared almost overnight in favor of inexpensive religious pamphlets and public posters printed in German.

The spread of printing to the north geographically expanded Luther's influence and, conversely, ensured support of his movement in the northern territories. The shift from scholarly books to mostly propagandist tracts of the pamphlets limited, although it did not restrict, access to the more diverse and secular knowledge of Greek and Latin classics, works from the natural sciences, humanist literature, and so forth. However, the introduction and mass utilization of the vernacular, both high and low German, facilitated the spread of the word to more people than ever before. Cheap access to pamphlets printed in the people's language coupled with Luther's insistence on the importance of learning to read in order to study the scriptures, brought an unlettered laity in direct visual contact with their own language while inculcating them with new ideas they had hitherto probably not seriously considered. Reading was no longer confined to the formally educated, the affluent, or those competent in Latin, but the printed word reached the households of the poor, the rural, as well as middle and lower class urban burghers. Protestant teachings about the new faith, family relations, childrearing, and children's education spread rapidly and widely on the material surface of the pamphlet literature.

Luther's Publications

Luther's writings were primarily sermons, addresses, and short treatises published in pamphlet form. His two major literary works were a German, that is Lutheran, version of the Bible (New Testament: 1522; Old Testament: 1534), and his translation of the Psalms (1531).

We begin in 1517 with the posting of Luther's ninety-five theses on the portals of the Wittenberg castle church. The theses were entitled "A Sermon on Indulgences and Grace." The posting of events, commentaries or complaints on the castle door was not an uncommon practice. Luther, however, was not posting just another theological commentary but was, indeed, posting an event in the true sense of the word. The theses were Luther's response to John Tetzel, a Dominican friar, who had been commissioned by Pope Leo X to sell thousands of indulgences in Germany in order to raise the necessary funds for rebuilding St. Peter's Cathedral in Rome. Febvre and Martin note that "his theses, translated into German and summarized, were printed as flysheets and distributed throughout Germany; within 15 days they had been seen in every part of the country."[60]

The theses appeared under the Latin title *Disputatio pio Declaratione Virtutis Indulgentarium*, were published in Wittenberg in the winter of 1517, and were followed by three other editions, two published in Wittenberg and one in Nüremberg. In the following year, they were reedited and published in German in Wittenberg under the title *Solutions*.

Luther's famous *Address to the Christian Nobility of the German Nation*, printed in August of 1520, sold 5,000 copies in five days. That same year Luther published *Why the Books of the Pope and his Disciples were burnt by Dr. Martin Luther* in defense of his provocative book burning of papal decrees and law books — 1,400 copies of this pamphlet were sold at the Frankfurt Fair in two days.[61]

In September of 1522, Luther completed his German version of the New Testament, adding to nineteen already existing German editions of the Bible.[62] This first edition, printed at Wittenberg, produced 5,000 copies and in December a second edition issued another 5,000 copies.[63] This work was pirated and reprinted by the "enterprising" Petri of Basel "towards the close of that same year."[64] Putnam further notes that Petri printed seven more editions within the following three years, another rival Basel printer produced five more editions, and an Augsburg printer issued three editions. Febvre and Martin add to Putnam's account and note that the New Testament, "printed . . . on three presses working flat out . . . was sold out in about 10 weeks despite its comparatively high price."[65] One can assume that members of the faculty and the Wittenberg intelligentsia purchased many copies of the first editions, despite the high cost. Between 1522 and 1524, fourteen more editions were printed at Wittenberg and sixty-six editions printed at other German presses.

Translation of the Old Testament was a joint effort of Luther and his former pupil and colleague Philip Melanchthon; the first German translations appeared in 1534. Some 430 authorized editions of Luther's translation came off the presses before 1546; pirated editions without the author's name appeared throughout Germany—one pirated edition ran to 3,000 copies. Dedicated to the Lutheran cause, printer Hans Lufft issued 100,000 copies of the Bible within forty years between 1534 and 1574. Febvre and Martin estimate that a total of one million German Bibles was printed before mid-century, and more than one million printed during the latter part of the century.[66]

People were buying Bibles in unprecedented numbers—a Bible in every household was Luther's aim to which the public responded with obvious enthusiasm. "The Scriptures were henceforth in everyone's hands and the passions roused by religious controversy were such that even those who were illiterate had the text read to them by better educated friends."[67] Putnam explains the intellectual and practical relevance of Luther's version of the New Testament:

> The complete Lutheran version of The New Testament . . . constituted not only . . . a central fact of first importance in the work of the Reformation, but the most noteworthy of the literary productions of its author. The work is of necessity classed as a translation, but it was a translation into which had been absorbed, in very large measure, the individuality and original thought of the writer. . . . The teaching that Christian believers must base their relations with their Creator upon the inspired Word required that this Word should be placed within reach of all Christians and should be in a form to be understood by the unlettered as well as the scholarly.[68]
> scholarly.[68]

Towards the end of the 1520s, Luther's publications appeared less frequently in both Latin and German versions. More pamphlets in high and low German were printed concerned less with scholarly doctrinal polemics, and more focused on didactic moralizing on everyday issues such as the choice of marriage partner, conduct in marriage, childrearing, and children's education. These shorter pamphlets, written in simple language and in regional dialects, appealed to a wider audience including the poor and barely literate. Since these pamphlets were small and lightweight in comparison to books, they were easily transportable and reached communities far from the centers of the urban book trade.

That large parts of rural Germany were still illiterate or semi-literate in the early decades of the century, was perceived as no obstacle by Luther and his followers. Luther envisioned the perfect Christian household as one where the family gathered in the evenings to listen to and discuss readings from the scriptures; if parents do not possess the skills of reading, "let the boys read to their parents every-day an article from the catechism and also sing them a song or two."[69] Luther's intent here is twofold: first, to instill in the young the daily practice of dealing with the words of God whether through song, prayer, reading or recitation and, second, to encourage whomever has the ability to read to gather members of the family or community for group instruction in the holy words. Towards the end of the century, "nearly everywhere regulations required children to share with their parents the fruits of their learning."[70] And, as Strauss points out, the il-literacy in sixteenth century Germany has been historically overrated:

> the ability to read with fair fluency was evidently much more widespread in 16th century German society than is ordinarily recognized.[71]

Literacy, the Peasantry, and Revolution

The recovery, translation, and correction of the texts of antiquity dur-ing the first fifty years of printing laid out a revised foundation of knowledge for European scholars. The uses to which the revised classics were put depended upon, as much as they precipitated, a changed outlook. The errors uncovered by scholars, not only semantic but factual errors, were being substantiated by practitioners: navigators, physicians, astronomers, merchant-explorers, mathematician-account-ants, teachers, and so forth.

Printing enabled the rapid reproduction of revised and new knowledge; knowledge encoded in books made ideas, literally, por-table, and liberated ideas from the guarded, locked up and inaccessi-ble manuscript scrolls in monastic and university libraries. Printing changed intellectual work from the solitary activity of medieval scholarship into a cooperative and international knowledge industry. At the same time, however, printing individualized learning by gradually eliminating the necessity for students to copiously recite and transcribe entire lectures, or copy from library manuscripts; printing freed the scholar's memory from the task of recording and retaining a vast stock of ideas of encyclopedic proportions. Conversely, for the reader converted to the Lutheran faith who was neither a cleric nor scholar, reading the Bible, catechisms, or prayer books encouraged communal learning and interaction. The ideal situation in Luther's view was for family and community members to gather together and listen to the reading of the holy words by those who were literate; discussion and group interaction would follow to further reinforce a sense of family and community spirit, and to promote ideological and social cohesion. We must remember that reading print in the sixteenth century was not silent reading but reading aloud to oneself or to an audience of listeners. So, inasmuch as print privatized text learning,[72] under early Protestantism popular printed literature (i.e., religious works) also promoted a collective learning, or a "brotherhood" of oral readers.

By the sixteenth century, Italian humanist values and ideas had spread northward. Antiquity, so long forgotten and buried in an "age of darkness" following the decline of Rome, was seen by the humanists in a new light; they viewed their own age as a new epoch—an age of enlightened curiosity and tolerance. Rewriting the past with a sense of a particularized and visibly different present, gave men and women a new sense of history, one not inseparably linked to the history of Christendom, but one seen in relationship to classical art, poetry, architecture, music, and sculpture. A critique of the inherited legacy of classical knowledge was part of a more general skepticism towards old and outmoded institutions grown rigid and resistant to change. And so, in the early translations of the Testaments and the classics, a subtle secularization and textual criticism marked the rewriting of history. This "Renaissance spirit"—of the urge to rediscover the past, to critically reevaluate and broaden, that is, secularize explanations of a forgotten past—characterized the intellectual tenor already widespread and firmly rooted in the attitude and outlook of the educated class of Western Europe by the time the first Bible was produced by Gutenberg in 1452.

The preceding section has sketched the development of printing from 1450 to the end of the sixteenth century, and discussed some of the implications of printing for the spread of literacy, the rise of Protestantism, and the popularization of secular and religious ideas about childrearing. The availability and distribution of print information during the first fifty years of printing advanced literacy and, reciprocally, a more widespread print literacy generated increased demand for printed literature. It can be argued, as Luther did, that the popularization of literacy was socially and politically dangerous. Certainly the social, ideological, and political changes that Luther instigated are attributable, at least in part, to his calculated use of the new print technology. Yet the political and socioeconomic conditions of sixteenth century central and northern Europe, and of Germany in particular, were oppressive and intolerable for the masses and cannot be overlooked as antecedent conditions ripe for radical change. Along with the advent of printing, deteriorating political and economic conditions in early sixteenth century Germany are concomitant factors underlying the threshold of change from which and because of which the Protestant Reformation emerged.

The sixteenth century inherited a two-century heritage of technical inventions and intellectual creativity, as well as a growing civic and theological dissatisfaction with church doctrine and church politics. Populations in Europe increased steadily during the fourteenth and fifteenth centuries, and by the sixteenth century a relatively large population of middle class burghers and peasants was a potentially powerful political force to be reckoned with.

By 1500, the population of Germany, the largest country in Europe, had risen to twenty million people.[73] Less than one million people lived in major metropolitan centers and large towns; more than nineteen million lived in villages, hamlets, and small towns with populations under 1,000. Overpopulation increased the economic burden of peasants for whom there was increasingly less land on which to raise livestock and crops. Unable to make a profit by selling surplus food, peasants found themselves unable to pay ever increasing taxes. This resulted in the rise of an itinerant beggar population of "landless laborers and gardeners . . . [who] multiplied in the countryside."[74]

Population growth could no longer be absorbed by the agricultural economy, and cities were already considered overcrowded.[75] The prosperity and rising wealth enjoyed by small city-states was paralleled by increasing tension between landlord and tenant in rural areas. The subtle structural changes in production and the organization of labor coupled with the problems of overpopulation and an inefficient, outmoded food production system, widened the gap and increased the tension between rich and poor, between urban and rural, between labor and capital.[76] While the peasantry organized to overthrow the yoke of serfdom, city merchants organized to save their businesses from financial collapse in the face of monopoly expansion. Braudel notes that "in fact the word monopoly became a real battlecry in sixteenth century Germany."[77] In May and March of 1525, for instance, the "Nüremberg Reichstag pronounced against the giant firms but they were saved by two edicts in their favor issued by the Emporer Charles V."[78] Throughout urban and rural Germany, organized and still peaceful resistance to secular and ecclesiastical power was repeatedly defeated "on paper."

It is against this economic and political backdrop, which had developed into crisis proportion by the 1520s, that Reformation ideology emerged at times triumphant, at others embattled. The following description of the events of the 1520s explains the plight of the common folk; from this we may better understand and appreciate the perceived need for and consequences of the educational reform movement of the mid-century that is the focus of the next chapter.

To keep a restless, dependent and disenfranchized peasantry immobilized and depoliticized, heavy taxation served both to maintain ruling landlords and clergy, and to keep peasants, physically, "in their place." Fees were implemented in many villages throughout the territories to discourage wanderers and newcomers. Intermarriage between individuals of politically distinct territories as severely taxed, children could be disinherited by law, or such marriages were prohibited outright by law. Property taxes, death taxes, inheritance taxes, excise taxes, imperial taxes to support the Turkish wars, ecclesiastical taxes, taxes on wine and beer, meat and flour, exemplify only partially the kind of financial demands made on peasants by "the tyrants and bloodsuckers," as one contemporary put it.[79]

Peasant grievances against taxation, against their diminishing fishing and hunting rights, the regulations prohibiting the cutting of timber, the restrictions of grazing rights on local commons and meadows, and their objections to compulsory labor for the local church and lordships were longstanding prior to 1525. In the early months of 1525, *The Twelve Articles* of the Upper Swabian peasants was printed as a list of all such grievances. In March, twenty-five editions of *The Twelve Articles* were published, producing some 25,000 copies that were disseminated throughout large sections of the southern German empire.[80]

> Like a parabolic mirror, the *Twelve Articles* collected and focused the grievances of Upper Swabian villages, and multiple reprintings made the crisis of the agragarian order clear to peasants of the whole empire.[81]

The publications of Luther's works between 1517 and 1525 cannot be said to have triggered or caused the ensuing peasant revolt, but they did contribute to the peasants' sense of justification for their demands. Godly law, according to Luther, to be found in clear and unambiguous terms in the Bible, underscored the peasants' demand to break with territorial interpretation of "ecclesiastical law"; peasants called for a just community of a Christian brotherhood under godly law as laid out in the scriptures. Natural law, Luther preached, was godly law to which each individual had an equal right and equal access by reading the Bible. With scripture as the sole and final authority over individual and communal secular and spiritual life, the legitimacy of a political and social order dictated by church law and interpreted by ruling lords was broken.

Underlying Luther's theology was an "individual equality before God" ethic which both peasant and urban burgher understood and used, albeit to dissimilar ends. Luther's teachings emphasized the teaching of a "pure" gospel, unmediated by the rites of sacraments or communion, and he encouraged communities to select their own pastor. On this basis, the old notion of the church as mediator between God and individual, and the church as administrative body of secular and spiritual affairs was rejected and replaced by the notion of a regional congregation—a Christian brotherhood of equals before God. This conceptual "democratization" of secular and spiritual life, as the peasantry understood it, meant equal and natural rights to God's worldly kingdom: the forests, streams, plants, and animals. The peasants' interpretation of Luther's teachings, however, proved to be erroneous in the eyes of Luther and ruling authorities.

Sporadic uprisings in central and southern Germany were already prevalent in 1524; by the spring of 1525 rebellion had spread throughout Germany. Mercenary troops ranging in number from 2,000 to 15,000 and peasants had set the country aflame.[82] H. Holborn estimates that in late April of 1525, 300,000 peasants were under arms, and the general estimate of the death toll for the years between 1524 and 1526 is around 100,000.

Luther, as many historians note, was shocked by the crisis. His siding with the nobility against the peasants is attributed to his misunderstandings of the peasants' interpretation of his own teachings; Luther had preached for reform, for Christian egalitarianism before God, not violence and mass civil disobedience. From the very beginning, Luther recognized the importance of maintaining congenial relationships with princes, dukes and electors, for here lay the real power that could support church reform. He nonetheless saw the equal importance of public support and, hence, could not tolerate the destruction of both sides on spiritual grounds, and the destruction of established authority on what can be considered political grounds.

The aftermath of the revolution saw the sharp decline in church authority and the corresponding increase in state control. The reformed territories and imperial cities claimed jurisdiction from the church regime over law, education, and finance. Monasteries, cathedral chapters and the long established judicial authority of the church came under the rule of local courts and local-regional municipal law.[83]

It has been necessary to describe, somewhat broadly, the antecedent political conditions of the 1525 rebellion of which the educational reform movement of the subsequent decade was one of several consequences. The developments of constitutional and civil rights reform after the 1525 revolution were not exclusively dominated by the "spirit of Lutheranism," but did influence and modify the changes underway throughout central and northern Europe, and Germany in particular. It is against the aftermath of the social, political, and economic upheavals of the late 1520s and early 1530s that we now look specifically at the educational reform considered by Luther and his followers to be an essential first step and precondition for greater social reform towards the envisioned social order of a Christian brotherhood — a priesthood of all believers.

The following chapter examines the works of Luther and his contemporaries who were concerned with educational reform; men who were greatly influenced by Luther's new theology and translated his ideas into educational practice. This discourse — the reformers' writings and practical innovations — reveals ideas about childhood that were influenced, in part, by the ideals of classical humanism and the ideals of what was to be known as Protestantism.

4

Lutheran Pedagogical Principles

Developments Prior to School Reform

The peasant rebellion changed Luther's attitude towards the German people, and his perceptions of the influence and consequences of his own work. The religious and social chaos of the previous years had led to deterioration and, in some cases, total disintegration of church and school. What was desperately needed was a thorough assessment and documentation of existing conditions from which a scheme for the reorganization of church, school, and community could be derived. In 1527 Luther, with the support of the Elector of Saxony, launched the first civil church-school survey. Luther's personal friend and colleague at Wittenberg, Philip Melanchthon, wrote the *Instructions to the Visitors* (1528) that was to guide examiners in their visitations to every parish of the territory.[1] The *Instructions*, then, formalized and set the surveillance techniques of Lutheran pedagogy into motion. Ideas about the education of the young, initially surfacing in the prescriptive discourse of Luther's pamphlets which urged parents to send their children to school, now reemerged in a discourse that was to serve as an observational template for educatonal authorities in their surveillance of schools. Visitations were undertaken to accumulate data on schools, teachers, communities, parents, and children; this data, in turn, was meant to lead to a complete overhaul of existing schooling practices.

The *Instructions* legitimated a large-scale surveillance network and extended the discursive practice of pedagogy to a further level of formalization. Not only were all children to be legally placed under the direct supervision and control of the school, but the school, its procedures, functions, and its schoolmasters were to come under the systematic scrutiny of regular visitations. The visitation authorities comprised a newly formed disciplinary hierarchy—not unlike the emergent disciplinary regime of magistrates, police officers, and jurists that Aries noted of seventeenth century France—which was concerned with both the public, institutional aspects of the school as well as with the private life of students, parents, and schoolmasters. The first territory in which visitations were systematically conducted was the Electorate of Saxony; the *Instructions* was soon adopted by other districts and by the 1560s all "reformed" pro-Lutheran territories throughout Germany had implemented territorial visitations.[2]

The future success of church and social reform was seen to lie with the young; the need to produce citizens who would be literate and conversant with religious doctrine, could best be achieved by mass schooling. And to assure the uniform transmission of a uniform body of knowledge and values, civil authorities cast a close net of surveillance in the form of school ordinances and visitations to control students, teachers, and schools. The implementation of compulsory school attendance laws, the reorganization of curriculum, instruction, teacher training, and student classification according to age-grade levels and examination results, converged in the systematic establishment of (early) "modern" public schooling. Luther's interpretation of doctrine was the source and motivation for the comprehensive educational reorganization which, in the course of several decades, changed the routines of children's lives. Along with the institutionalization of text learning, childhood became institutionalized. The discourse on childhood no longer resided in the more informal texts of household, conduct, or pediatric guides, but passed the threshold of formalization by its transformation into institutionalized, discursive practices that were legitimated and enforced by compulsory school attendance laws.

The church-school survey revealed what appeared to Luther as a serious and widespread lack of commitment by parents to send their children to school. Formerly, the study of the learned disciplines assured boys a future in the priesthood or the professions, "but these livings were swept away in the revolution which was now taking place."[3] As a result, local schools and universities "were deserted," since "parents refused to have their sons study for a vocation so uncertain."[4] Parents' negative attitude towards a formal education was further reinforced by the reformers' rejection of traditional scholarship, that is monastic learning which, in Luther's words "is really a lazy, secure, and good life."[5] As early as 1520, he had called for university reform in his *Address to the Christian Nobility* which, as noted in chapter 3, was an instant bestseller, selling 5,000 copies in five days. Condemning the universities, Luther wrote:

> What are the universities, as at present ordered, but, as the book of Maccabees says, "schools of 'Greek fashion' and 'heathenish manners'" . . . where . . . Aristotle rules even further than Christ?[6]

In addition, parental resistance to a formal education for their children may have been implicitly supported by the wide dissemination and availability of the vernacular Bible that Luther had claimed all along to hold the key to personal enlightenment and redemption. Why, then, send children to school when the most authoritative and important knowledge — the vernacular Bible — lay available in every household?

Yet, by the late 1520s, Luther very clearly saw the need for an educated civil service trained in the classical languages, in church and civil law, and history; facility only with German was considered insufficient for good church and state government. In his popular *Sermon on Keeping Children in School* he explains:

> Every community, and especially a great city, must have in it many kinds of people besides merchants. It must have people who can do more than simply add, subtract and to read German. German books are made primarily for the common man to read at home. . . . There may, of course, be an occasional idolator, . . . who will take his son out of school and say, "If my son can read and do arithmetic, that is enough; we now have books in German, etc." Such a person sets a bad example for all the other good citizens.[7]

Ten years earlier, in his *Address to the Christian Nobility* Luther had judged the study of the classical disciplines and languages to be useful to men "of higher understanding":

> Aristotle's books on Logic, Rhetoric, and Poetry, should be retained . . . in a condensed form. Besides this, there are the languages — Latin, Greek, and Hebrew — the mathematics, history; which I recommend to men of higher understanding.[8]

Luther initially accepted as natural the inequality of men in the "worldly kingdom" — the rich and poor, the "common man," and the "men of higher understanding." His views of governance of the worldly kingdom changed after the peasant revolt and his subsequent participation in one of the visitations, to include the "middle class of common people." In 1525 he wrote in reply to the peasants' *Twelve Articles*:

> A worldly kingdom cannot exist without an inequality of persons, some being free, some imprisoned, some lord, some subjects, etc.[9]

Five years later, in 1530, he wrote:

> It is not God's will that only those who are born kings, princes, lords, and nobles should exercise rule and lordships. He wills to have his beggars among them also, lest they think it is nobility of birth rather than God alone who makes lords and rulers.[10]

Giving his own background and schooling as an example for the necessity of sending children to school, he continues:

> Without any doubt, I should not have come to this if I had not gone to school and become a writer. Therefore go ahead and send your son to study . . . your son and my son, that is, the children of the common people, will necessarily rule the world, both in the spiritual and worldly estates. . . . The born princes and lords cannot do it alone . . . Thus both kinds of government on earth must remain with the middle class of common people.[11]

Schooling for professions in church and state government was no longer reserved for the privileged elite but was, in principle, open to and encouraged for the "everyman" of the common people.

Upon return from a visitation in November, 1528, Luther "was profoundly moved by the dense ignorance and indifference, gross immorality and spiritual destitution which prevailed everywhere."[12] Henceforth, he would favor Latin over vernacular schools. Luther recognized that a broader, partially classical education was essential for the training of future church and state leaders. Melanchthon took over the redesigning of the Latin school curriculum and Luther took charge of reforming the curriculum of existing vernacular schools. That winter Luther set himself to work writing the *Short Catechism* and the *Longer Catechism*.[13] Both works were to replace the Bible in religious school instruction in the hope that a summarized and short version of Christian doctrine would preclude individual misinterpretation. In the preface of the *Small Catechism* he explained:

> The miserable and deplorable situation that I myself encountered during my recent journeys as a visitor has forced and compelled me to cast this catechism, that is, the Christian doctrine, in such a small, concise and simple form.[14]

Both works went to press in early 1529. As the data collected from the church-school surveys showed, parents could not be trusted to raise children in an appropriate Christian manner, let alone be trusted to voluntarily send their children to school. The next imperative step was to expand and enforce universal and compulsory education. Compulsory schooling had already been implemented in Magdeburg, a city not far from Wittenberg, in 1524 and in Eisleben, Luther's birthplace, in 1525.[15] In 1528, compulsory schooling came under civil law in the Electorate of Saxony, in which Wittenberg was located.[16]

On Marriage, Family, and Children

Luther's view on education was inextricably linked to his understanding of doctrine. But he was also deeply influenced by the ideas of his lifelong friend Melanchton who, unlike Luther, was committed to humanist scholarship. Luther, on the other hand, was first and foremost a theologian in all that he wrote, and acted upon throughout his life. And it was Melanchton who became the de facto author of Luther's school reform movement; Luther himself can be considered more of a publicist of their combined ideas.

The fourth commandment, "Honor thy father and thy mother," was the foundational dictum upon which Luther's notion of a sound family, an orderly community, and a Christian society was based. Partially in response to his own allegedly harsh upbringing and his long harbored grief over the unsatisfactory relationship with his father,[17] Luther advocated parental tolerance, and a more judicious use of corporal punishment than he had experienced in his own childhood.

> In vigorous language he censured laxity in parental control and faulty methods of training. On the other hand, he frowned upon undue severity. In his childhood home he had suffered deeply from the harshness of his parents, yet he held them in the highest respect and veneration through all his days. He loved his own children tenderly, and a more natural, happy family relationship can scarcely be imagined.[18]

Luther was no "armchair" theologian-pedagogue. One June 13, 1525, he married a former nun. Marriage of the clergy was prohibited by canon law, yet clandestine relationships had long been accepted practice among priests. Luther and others recognized that the clergy were not true to their vows of celibacy and that many "lived in concubinage in return for a yearly tax paid to the bishop."[19] In his *Address to the Christian Nobility*, written five years prior to his marriage, Luther justified clerical marriage by reference to scripture:

> We see also how the priesthood is fallen, and how many a poor priest is encumbered with a woman and children and burdened in his conscience, and no one does anything to help him, though he might very well be helped . . . every town should have a minister or bishop, as St. Paul plainly says (Titus i.), and this minister should not be forced to live without a lawful wife, but should be allowed to have one.[20]

Luther's views of marriage and of children were profoundly effected by his own domestic experience; his wife bore six children. Upon the death of his first daughter Elizabeth, Luther wrote to a friend:

> My little daughter is dead. I am left as weak as a woman. I would never have believed that the hearts of parents are so moved towards children.[21]

In *Tischreden* (Table Talk), Luther comments on family life and children:

> Nothing is more sweet than harmony in marriage, and nothing more distressing than dissention. Next to it is the loss of a child. I know how that hurts. . . . Marriage offers the greatest sphere for good works, because it rests on love — love between the husband and wife, love of the parents for the children, whom they nourish, clothe, rear, and nurse. If a child is sick, the parents are sick with worry.[22]

The death of children was not an uncommon experience for parents rich or poor. And as Strauss notes,

> any suggestion that people in former ages took less pleasure in their children than we do in ours, or felt less pity for their pains and grief at their death, ignores the testimony of the sources.[23]

Contrary to Aries' claims of parental indifference to children, the sentiments expressed by Luther over the loss of his daughter reflect strong affective ties between parent and child.[24] Moreover, Luther's feelings and views were shared by other contemporaries.

Fellow reformer John Oecolampadius (Johannes Huszgen), a minister, scholar of Greek and Hebrew, professor of theology at Basel, and friend of Erasmus whom he had helped prepare the publication of the New Testament, was one of the first to follow Luther's example of clerical marriage.[25] Oecolampadius' first child, a son, was apparently a sickly infant; in a letter to a friend we note Oecolampadius' concern about the boy:

> Eusebius is a gentle and quiet child unless hungry, thirsty or in need of change. He is very subject to colds and coughing. I fear he will not live long.[26]

Eusebius died at age 13. Of Philip Melanchthon, one of his biographers writes:

Melanchthon was attached to his children with deep love. Visitors sometimes saw him with a book in his hand, sitting at the baby's cradle.[27]

Similar parental control and caring is expressed in a letter by Luther addressed to his wife written in 1532:

I can't find any suitable presents for the children in this town, although it is the annual fair. See if you can dig up something at home for me to give them.[28]

Pediatrician Otto Brunfels in *Weiber und Kinder Apothek* (Women and Children's Apothecary) published in 1535, advised parents:

Parents should be kind to their children and give them their attention at all times.[29]

In 1545, Caspar Huberinus published the two volume *Postilla Teutsch* (German Postil) in which he reminds parents that:

Children are God's gift to husbands and wives. Parents should truly love and cherish such divine treasures, raising and keeping them to the best of their ability in constant remembrance of God's benevolence.[30]

The above letters reveal emotional responses to personal experience; they show us sensitive concerns and affection for children of well-educated and prominent fathers. Parallel to the formal pedagogic discourse — school ordinances and curricula — the more private discourse of correspondence authored by fathers indicates that concern for children was not primarily theologically motivated rhetoric aimed at bringing the nation's children under social and thought control. Clearly these expressed sentiments provide counter-evidence for fathers' alleged indifference towards children, and such testimony also does not support the stereotype of the straight-laced, cold-hearted paternal image of the sixteenth century father. Yet here, the lack of sources with which to document another point of view — that of mothers and wives — limits historical investigation.

The missing link in the reconstruction of historical childhoods lies with those most familiar and knowledgeable of the routine upbringing of children: women as mothers, wetnurses, nursemaids, or governesses. De jure authority over matters pertaining to household affairs, education, community, and society lay in the hands of men who, given the rigid division of household labor in the sixteenth century, could not claim de facto authority — knowledgeable authority through experience or paticipation — over the routine labors of childrearing. Yet the literature abounds with a wide array of male expertise on every topic concerning women's conduct, children's conduct, how to breastfeed, swaddle and wean, how to punish and how to reward, what to teach, how to teach, and how to learn. Perhaps many more fathers than is commonly assumed actively participated in the upbringing of their children.

The affectionate concern for children expressed in the privacy of personal correspondence, and the attention paid to children in pediatric and household guides, do not reflect indifference to childhood, but reflect the importance adults placed on parental kindness, love, and attention. The aforementioned examples seem to indicate a greater sympathy and concern for children than many historians — notably Aries, Stone, and DeMause — are willing to recognize. And so we turn from the emotional responses of prominent fathers to domestic concerns, to an examination of how their private attitudes towards their own children differed from or reflected in the formulation of their pedagogical theories.

On Infancy

Humankind, according to Luther, is born into sin. In the infant, "original sin is as deep-seated as it is in the adult. In the child it lies dormant, not ready to reveal itself in overt actions."[31] Childish innocence, then, is no more than a transitory developmental stage within which sinful impulses have not yet become self-conscious and recognizable to the child. As Luther put it in 1535:

> they [children] know no sin, they live without greed, . . . they will take an apple as cheerfully as a coin.[32]

Both Luther and Melanchthon rejected the Aristotelean notion of infantile minds as "blank slates" upon which experience records impressions. Instead, both believed that evil and sin are universal and innate propensities which, unless tempered early by parental guidance and discipline, would reveal themselves in immoral, sinful conduct. Luther explained:

> Children under seven years of age have not developed real
> thoughts. We know this because they do not feel the urge to
> kill and commit adultery. Still, sin has begun to stir within, as
> is evident in their tendency to steal sweets, and so on.[33]

Many of Luther's contemporaries, such as the German pediatrician Metlinger, the Spanish humanist and "father of modern psychology" Juan Luis Vives, and Erasmus, did not share Luther's ideas
about innate sin, but considered infants as neutral, "crude matter."
Believing in the inheritance of sin, Luther and Melanchthon saw home
and school discipline as the only and most effective means of com-
bating innate sinful tendencies. Through an understanding of scripture, the attainment of faith, and a life in "the service of one's
neighbour," the individual could hope to counterbalance, but never
overcome, the essential feature of the human condition: the inheritance of original sin. From the negative thesis of inherited sin at
birth, the individual progresses through life towards the uncertain
promise of salvation and eternal life after death — the positive thesis of
possible redemption. This position Melanchthon and Luther, who had
been trained as an Augustinian monk, shared with Saint Augustine,
who in the *Confessions*, had laid the foundation for the doctrine of
predestination. In Book I of his autobiographical recollections, Augustine rejects innocence in infancy and claims that individuals are born
into sin and guilt; as he put it, "in sin did my mother conceive me."[34]
Augustine viewed the mind as predisposed with sinful ideas and
tendencies with which sense impressions associate. Mind, Augustine
explains, holds "generic" ideas and concepts that become self-
conscious in their substance and form through sensory experience. For
instance, a signifying sound, emotion, or images of "things themselves," bring forth uncoded ideas or concepts from memory and en-
dow them with a particular set of defining characteristics. How could
one learn or know of things.

> unless they were already in the memory, but so thrown back
> and buried as it were in deeper recesses, that had not the sug-
> gestion of another drawn them forth I had perchance been
> unable to conceive of them?[35]

Luther's concept of human nature bearing a legacy of inherited
sin is a direct derivation from Augustine's teachings. If the human
condition, the human mind, and individual destiny is so seen, then
there can be, in theory, no innocence in childhood. Moreover, the

possibility for a concerted effort to instill in individuals and society at large, habits of self-discipline with which to control the everpresent influence of Satan, was seen to lie naturally with home and school training of still impressionable young minds. From birth to approximately age seven, children's reason is "asleep"; hence, they cannot be held accountable for sinful acts. And because children's reason is not fully developed during the first seven years, this is an ideal time for parents to inculcate sound Christian moral values. With the awakening of reason children would be capable of intentional disobedience to God and to parents at which time, however, the school would intervene with more rigorous moral training and discipline.

Luther's own upbringing and schooling were apparently severe and left a lasting impression. Luther's childhood experience may very well have prompted Luther to call for more moderate disciplinary measures in the treatment of children, although he never ceased to agree with the equal need for "rule by the rod." As an Augustinian monk, Luther was well familiar with all of Augustine's works; it is not implausible that Luther identified his own childhood memories in St. Augustine's writings. Augustine, recalling the beatings he received as a schoolboy from his masters when "we sinned in writing or reading or studying less than was expected of us," remembers the use of "racks and hooks and other torments."[36] He justifies such punishment as a legitimate means of curtailing children's frivolous play at the expense of study, and sympathizes with adults who must punish children for their own good. Parents and teachers desire what is best for children even if the attainment of goals, the precondition of which is study, necessitates severe punishment:

> almost all wish the same for their children, and yet are very willing that they should be beaten, if those very games detain them from their studies.[37]

Rejecting infants' innocence, Augustine observed natural sinful tendencies manifest in behavior even before the child can speak:

> I have myself seen jealousy in a baby and know what it means. He was not old enough to talk, but whenever he saw his foster-brother at the breast, he would grow pale with envy.[38]

Early childhood, then, was seen by Augustine and Luther as critical for the formation of virtuous attitudes and behaviors to stem the tide of immoral impulses which would, at age seven, develop into "real thoughts." If the school was to take over training of the young at age seven, the pedagogical methods of formal teaching would have to rely much on the quality of preparatory instruction given children in the home. The preschooler, if properly raised at home, should have acquired the necessary self-discipline with which to recognize and combat corrupt ideas in the self and in others, once formal schooling begins. And how else to instill self-discipline than through the use of discipline?

The reformulation by Luther of Augustinian doctrine exemplifies what Foucault considers the transposition of intact or modified concepts from historically preceding or contemporaneous discourses which, in their modified rearticulation on a new field of emergence, inscribe ideas in between or adjunct to existing discourses. An emergent discourse, even if it borrows concepts from antecedant or concurrent discourses, is "a unity of another type," which does not share the same date of origin as the "original" concept, and does not have the same surface of emergence, nor mode of articulation.[39] Saint Augustine's doctrine of original sin was rearticulated by Luther but given a new twist: certainly humanity was born into worldly conditions that tempted individuals to act upon innately sinful impulses. But, unlike Saint Augustine, Luther reconceptualized innate sin by uncoupling procreation from evil and sin, and by proposing that authentic individual faith could, quite successfully, counteract Mammon's ever-present influence. Moreover, by granting legitimacy to the holy estate of matrimony, to the earthly estate of family and community, Luther elevated the site of the everyday from one associated by Augustine with sin and corrupt vices, to one where the spirituality of the heavenly kingdom had its natural counterpart.

Luther's decidedly Augustinian doctrine, then, cannot be seen to share the same date of origin, form of articulation, or surface of emergence as that of Augustine's writings. Whereas Augustine's work circulated in restricted manuscript form among a literate male elite, Luther's writings surfaced in the public domain and circulated in multiple copies of vernacular German among men and women of the peasant, burgher, and aristocratic classes. As Foucault insists, not all discourses and discursive practices emerge without historical precedent but, often, emerge in juxtaposition to ideas and concepts enunciated and organized elsewhere; Luther's reworking of Saint Augustine's conceptualization of original sin, in Foucault's terms, can be considered as an emergent discourse positioned in relations of complementarity and succession to Augustine's discourse. Luther's theological and educational program for social and political reform conceptually modified and extended Augustine's notion of original sin, transposing this modification into a new discursive unity, and situating it into the sixteenth century socio-politico-religious discourse which subsumed the discourses on childhood, the family, and pedagogy.

"Perhaps the time has come," Foucault suggests, that we look beyond "the expressive value and formal transformations of discourse," and question instead

> its mode of existence: the modifications and variations, . . . modes of circulation, valorization, attribution and appropriation. . . . Where does it [discourse] come from; how is it circulated; who controls it?[40]

The sixteenth century Protestant discourse on childhood, embedded within concentric discursive layers surrounding the child—the family, the community, the school, the church—cannot be seen as a simple linear appropriation by Luther of Augustinian notions of sin: the fallen and irredeemable infant whose greed for milk at the breast betrays a wicked infantile sinfulness. The intent of tracing Luther's concept of sin to Saint Augustine is not to establish relations of causality on the continuum of the "progress of ideas." The archeologist reaches back in history not to determine, once and for all, a "founding figure" or the genesis of an idea, but traces the historical meanderings and transformations of concepts as they weave in and out of dominant and marginal discourses, and discursive practices. At a very general level, archeology is a morphological strategy that seeks out "the changing structure of diverse phenomena"; the historical method advocated by Foucault requires the archeologist to go back in time until a difference is located.[41]

Such difference is evident in the reconceptualization by Luther of the Augustinian concept of original sin; Saint Augustine's formulation of innate sin and predestination in *The Confessions* similarly marks an historical difference in relation to theological discourses predating and contemporaneous with fourth century thought. Far from seeking historical causality or a progressive continuity, an archeology of discourse establishes historical links and transformations by illuminating difference within relations of opposition as well as complementarity, parallelism, or succession. Reformation ideas about adolescence underwent similar transformations as those of childhood: succeeding, complementing, yet differing from earlier conceptualizations.

On Adolescence

The "classifications of childhood and youth into the three periods of 'infantia,' 'puerita,' and 'adolescentia' were ancient" and were not, contrary to Aries' claims, an eighteenth century invention; nor was adolescence "until the eighteenth century confused with childhood."[42] If anything, in premodern times, early or mid-adolescence marked the end of childhood for children of the peasantry at least who joined the adult world of work at home, in the fields, or as apprentices as early as eight or ten years of age.[43]

Reformation pedagogues reclassified adolescents from being considered as young adults, to adolescents as older children. Childhood was indeed extended to include adolescence, and this was accomplished by the establishment of a universal and compulsory program of institutionalized study, the completion of which would require attendance until age sixteen or eighteen.

The reformers of the sixteenth century based their opinions on youth on an established body of classical literature about childhood and adolescence. Luther, as already noted, drew many of his theological and pedagogical principles from Saint Augustine. Melanchthon, scholar of Latin, Greek and Hebrew was well familiar with the educational treatises of Cicero and Quintilian, upon whose works Erasmus based his educational theory.[44] Plato's pedagogy and social theory, Aristotle's developmental theory, and Socrates' dialogic method of instruction, were well-known by all Renaissance scholars, these authors having formed a substantial part of their own classical studies. In addition to those works the reformers studied as young men, the vernacular translation and reinterpretation of many of the classics, and the proliferation and access to numerous "contemporary" texts undoubtedly influenced their formulation of pedagogical principles and practices. Statements circulating in texts accessible to the reformers along with the practical questions to which they sought solutions, together influenced, mediated and shaped the ideas—including the revival of the already enunciated—of Reformation discourses.

Concerns about education swept throughout Europe in the sixteenth century, prompting the writing of a variety of popular and educational tracts. Theologians, scholars, and reformers sought to link traditional wisdom with a modern, religiously based understanding of contemporary social and educational needs. The circulation of ideas in books enabled communities of scholars to gain access to and communicate a diversity of ideas in a relatively short period of time. Ideas from antiquity influenced the modern pedagogue, and the rapidity with which modern ideas were disseminated through the printed word, led to speedier developments of disputes or agreements on practical or theoretical ussues often in the course of a year or two, sometimes within only months as, for instance, the disputation—in print—between Luther and Erasmus on the question of free will.

The development of educational theories during the sixteenth century, then, was as much a reworking of traditional sources as it was a product of the exchange of ideas between contemporary authors. Many of the educational ideas of antiquity were adopted by Reformation pedagogues who incorporated contemporary religious explanations for the teaching of foundational subjects such as logic, rhetoric, music, or the study of the ancient languages themselves.

Seven year developmental cycles, to which Luther adhered, appear fairly consistently in the educational theories of antiquity.[45] Formal training in classical Greece and Rome, whether at home by fathers, tutors, or at school, generally began between ages five to seven. Between age seven and mid-adolescence, children were seen to require systematic instruction; mid-adolescence appears to have been demarcated equally as either the beginning of adulthood through entrance into state service, or as the last phase of childhood requiring a more rigid form of intellectual and physical training. Age twenty-one generally marked full and legitimate entry into the adult world.

The classification of adolescence was not uniformly resolved during antiquity or during medieval times. The children of the common masses were never seen to require formal education under Hellenic or Roman rule, or in "barbarous" central and northern Europe at any time prior to the Reformation. The "revival of learning," spawned by the Italian Renaissance during the late fourteenth and fifteenth century, originated with and influenced the learning of an educated, affluent elite only. Humanist ideals alone perhaps would not have led to a call for public, mass education; but the need for state and church unity in the face of apparent moral and social decline in sixteenth century Germany, required a total reassessment of existing affairs and call for reform of the social order for which Luther became the spokesperson. And in the course of this reevaluation and redefinition of human "nature," human relations, and human destiny, all aspects of the human condition came under scrutiny, including adolescence.

Reflecting on his son's seventh birthday, Luther had this to say about the seven stages of the individual:

> My Hans is about to enter upon his seventh year, which is always climacteric, that is, a time of change. People always

change every seventh year. The first period of seven years is childhood, and at the second stage—say, in the fourteenth year—boys begin to look out into the world. . . . At the age of twenty-one youths desire marriage, in the twenty-eighth year young men are householders and heads of families, while at the age of thirty-five men have civil and ecclesiastical positions. This continues to the age of forty-two, when we are kings. Soon after this men begin to lose their sense. So every seventh year always brings to man some new condition and way of life. This has happened to me, and it happens to everybody.[46]

At roughly age fourteen, then, potential trouble begins to brew as "boys begin to look out into the world." One would expect, given Luther's concept of inherited sin, that the adolescent, at the developmental crossroads of childish ignorance and more elaborate cognitive abilities, would pose a particular problem in terms of the need to harness matured tendencies of sin and corruption. And, indeed, Luther and his contemporaries had much to say about the dangers that might befall adolescents unless self and external discipline was systematically and rigidly imposed. We find a parallel to Luther's thoughts on the natural yet sinful consequences of sexual maturation at puberty in Saint Augustine's *Confessions*. Remembering his adolescence with disdain, Augustine recalls the lies and thefts he committed, the vain and "unholy desires," the "muddy concupiscence of the flesh, . . . bubblings of youth, . . . the fog of lustfulness."[47] Such sins, he claimed, do not reflect any "innocence of boyhood," but attest to unbridled and inherent evil which, during puberty, ravage and mislead young boys. Augustine recalls the boyish tendencies which

did confusedly boil in me, and hurried my unstayed youth over the precipice of unholy desires, and sunk me into a gulf of flagitiousness.[48]

Luther agreed with Augustine that the awakening sexual desires in pubescent boys and girls could lead to the ruin of mind, body, and soul, unless brought under strict control. In the main, all sixteenth century "authors agreed that a more or less rigorous system of control was needed to keep boys of 14 and 15 from destroying themselves for life."[49]

Age fourteen, that second and very critical stage in Luther's seven year developmental theory posed particular psychosocial problems for boys and, hence, disciplinary problems for parents and teachers. Boys at fourteen were seen as sexually mature but, unlike girls, too immature to shoulder the responsibilities of married life. Comparing girls' and boy's maturity at age fourteen, Luther rather unfavorably compared them as "weeds" (girls) to "good crops" (boys):

> Girls begin to talk and stand on their feet sooner than boys because weeds always grow up more quickly than good crops. So girls who are fourteen years old are nubile, while boys of that age are not mature enough for marriage.[50]

Luther, incidentally, often metaphorically spoke of young children as young trees, malleable and still flexible; he equated obedient, pious children with "a sound tree" or "good fruit." Always cognizant that he was addressing the ordinary burgher in most of what he preached and wrote, these kinds of popular metaphors had broad appeal and helped him appear as one of the people, and for the people.

In 1500, the landmark book on adolescence was published in Strassburg, written in Latin by German humanist Jacob Wimpheling.[51] Wimpheling's *Adolescentia* typified the pubescent male as enslaved to "voluptuous desires that consume the body and mind."[52] The tensions of maturing sexuality manifest in "natural" vices such as:

> lying, blaspheming, violence and cruelty, theft, disobedience to parents and disrespect to their elders, idleness, gambling, restlessness, and lack of shame.[53]

As already noted, the authors of popular conduct manuals consistently warned of the dangers of leaving children and youths unsupervised who would fall prey to the evils of the street. The individual and social problems associated with adolescent and adult sexuality were of critical concern to Luther and his contemporaries. And the problem with sexuality was particularly difficult to resolve conceptually because the notion of original sin had cast the consequences of human sexuality into an eternal and permanent inheritance of immorality and sinful behaviors. Apart from sexual encounters within marriage for the sole purpose of procreation, most sexual activities were considered immoral deviations from conjugal duty conducted in "the fog of lustfulness." Yet sexuality was also considered a natural, divinely ordained aspect of human nature, as Luther points out:

> the marital act is not an act of concupiscence. Rather, the act which attracts sex to sex is a divine ordinance.[54]

Luther recognized that sexual urges are "more urgent than eating, drinking . . . sleeping and waking. It is rooted in us as part of our nature and species."[55] Celibacy, then, is unnatural and a rejection of God's divine ordinance; claiming chastity by taking eternal vows and then participating in clandestine sexual relationshps is a blasphemous consequence of an unnatural repressed sexuality. For, as Luther explains:

> We do not have the power to be voluntarily poor, obedient, or chaste. God alone can make that possible. Therefore, whoever makes this kind of a vow, pledges things that do not belong to him. In so doing, he blasphemes and despises God.[56]

Legitimating clerical marriage was one way to circumvent the unnatural and un-Christian practice and concept of chastity. A rejection of the principles of monastic vows was to help eliminate illicit sexual practices, and to legitimate and institutionalize them in the holy estate of matrimony. Luther's emphasis on the social and spiritual importance of the conjugal unit underscored the importance of marriage and the family; as well, his insistence on the need for less parental intervention in their children's choice of marriage partner, was meant to reduce the adulterous, sinful consequences of adolescent marriages of convenience. Luther's numerous and forceful indictments of the "false chastity" so characteristic of life in the monasteries and nunneries prompted countless men and women to leave the holy orders. Inasmuch as his own marriage to an escaped nun may have legitimated clerical marriage and helped liberate many women from cloistered confinement, his rejections of prearranged marriages undoubtedly saved many young girls from early domestic enslavement to household or childcare, or confinement in a cell enslaved in an illusory marriage to Christ.

By bringing adult sexuality within moral, legitimate and Christian boundaries, the irresistable power of sexuality could be given a natural and holy domain within which it could both flourish and be controlled. Civil marriage contracts, freedom of the clergy to marry, and an apparent freedom to choose one's mate were, indeed, revolutionary ideas and were seen by many Lutheran reformers as the key to curtail the need for sexual and social deviance: from doctrine, from God's will, and from natural biological impulses.

But what about early adolescent sexuality that was yet too immature to come under the sanction of matrimonial legitimation, yet too mature and potentially "dangerous" to be disregarded? The aim of

Reformation pedagogues was "not to eradicate sexual needs" — for all agreed on the divine yet double-edged nature of human sexuality — "but to postpone and, if possible, moderate them. Delayed sexual maturity would prolong the innocence of childhood."[57] And since, for Luther, childish innocence was not pure innocence, but more of a childish ignorance-innocence, then to postpone the consequences of sexual maturity could be achieved by prolonging children's isolation from the carnal knowledge of the street: by legally maintaining children in segregated schools and classes, under constant surveillance and control by school masters and institutional rules, and by means of an extended, uniform educational program based on discipline and regimentation.

Extending public schooling to include adolescence provided a moral alternative to the false chastity imposed upon many young girls and boys who, in previous centuries, had been consigned to ecclesiastical continence by their parents. As J. L. Flandrin notes, "the early medieval church prescribed marrying children soon after puberty because it thought it very difficult or even impossible to prevent young people from engaging in sexual activity."[58] Rejecting early and pre-arranged marriage, and the false chastity of monastic life, Lutheran reformers thought one alternative to celibacy or adolescent marriage to be prolonged and mandatory schooling, whereby juvenile sexuality could be more systematically surveilled and curtailed.

To instill piety, unmitigated faith and self-discipline in the individual was seen to require more than just the transmission of doctrinal ideas to the impressionable young. A truly Christian way of life, as the reformers envisioned it, would require the kind of disciplined training that in itself would mirror the quality of life children were expected to replicate upon reaching adulthood. Regularity and repetition were seen to be habit forming whereby conduct and ideas could be "drilled" into children, habituating them to what was learned by memorization and recitation. As Stone points out,

> The learning process was thought to rely heavily on the memory, so that repeated exercises and an orderly system of instruction were seen as the keys to successful pedagogy. . . . Religious and moral indoctrination through the installment of fixed habits were taken for granted as the prime purposes of education.[59]

Such methods were seen as ideal for moulding the very young and controlling adolescents who were considered to be under particular psychological stress. When left to their own devices, youths, as Melanchthon observed in 1537, were often raucous and unruly:

> Never were our youth so impatient of laws and of discipline,
> so determined to live after their own wills. . . . It is the part,
> not of men, but of Cyclops to make public tumults at night;
> to fill whole neighborhoods with furious outcries; to make
> bacchanalian and even hostile assaults upon the unarmed and
> innocent able citizens; to break in their doors and windows,
> destroy the slumbers of women in childbed, and of the wretched,
> the sick, and the aged; to demolish the booths in the market-
> place, carriages, and whatever else comes in the way.[60]

Melanchthon had hoped that schooling, which would "fill the hearts
of the young with the saving knowledge of God, of the nature of
things, and with good morals," might keep the young out of harm's
way.[61] As Strauss puts it, "young minds and bodies with time to kill
were easy prey for the devil."[62]

Repeatedly, all age levels of childhood, including adolescence,
came under the reformers' scrutiny. The principal assumption underlying the urgent calls for improved childcare by both home and school
was the common fear that without systematic temperance the human
predisposition to sin would unleash, even in children, in a torrent of
unbounded corruption and vice. The kind of senseless vandalism by
hooligan youths who "demolish the booths in the market-place, car-
riages, and whatever else comes in their way," as Melanchthon had
observed, confirmed the reformers' fears that without proper upbringing by home and school, youth would degenerate into lawless "Cy-
clops," devoid of civic or spiritual responsibility. The scenario envisioned by the reformers of undisciplined youth transformed into
adulthood bore even grimmer prospects. Only a firm discipline, instill-
ing in the young both a healthy fear and respect for God and adult
authority, would save future generations and save the nation. And as
much as Luther and others insisted on the importance of providing
children with love and affection, the need for obedience and discipline
was emphasized with equal importance.

Obedience and Discipline

Obedience to authority was considered a fundamental precondition
for adults and children alike, an indispensable attitude and behavior
requisite for acquiring true faith, for service to the state, and mandatory for the proper functioning of family and school. Inculcating
habits of submission was achieved in a number of ways. First, unques-

tioning obedience to and respect for parents was to be taught children from infancy. Secondly, it was hoped that extending schooling to include the years of adolescence and making schooling compulsory, would further expose and accustom children to a disciplined and structured way of life. Not only could the impressionable years of childhood be prolonged to include the years of puberty, but by keeping that potentially most troublesome age group occupied in schools and under the supervision of teachers, youths were, to some extent, detained from ruining themselves in the licentious atmosphere of the streets. Thirdly, as Strauss has noted, "the reformers' endeavors to imbue children with a sense of their innate depravity could be represented as a scheme for internalizing effective disciplinary constraints by using sin as an instrument of control."[63] Fear of God's wrath, the prospect of eternal hell and damnation, was undoubtedly a powerful and persuasive threat to stir children to obey not only the Ten Commandments, but to obey those rules of conduct set down by adults.

Preaching on the fourth commandment, Luther emphasized the importance of filial obedience to parents:

> Where this is not the case, you will find neither good manners nor good government. . . . For where obedience is not maintained at the fireside, no power on earth can ensure . . . the blessings of a good government. . . . If now the root is corrupt, it is in vain that you look for a sound tree or for good fruit.[64]

The root of corruption, original sin, is the inescapable human heritage which can, however, be tempered by "the parental estate God has especially honoured above all estates."[65] If children are neglected through parental indifference or incompetence, the worldly estate eventually deteriorates into the kind of social and moral decay Luther saw all around him. He warns fathers:

> No one should become a father unless he is able to instruct his children in the Ten Commandments and in the Gospel, so that he may bring up true Christians. But many enter the state of holy matrimony who cannot say the Lord's Prayer, and know nothing themselves, they are utterly incompetent to instruct their children."[66]

In the popular *Seelenführer* (Soul's Guide), published in 1498, the author addresses mothers and fathers calling for teaching by example, and attributes to the home the function of church and state:

> Let parents, therefore, be admonished to see that their chil-
> dren grow up in Christian fear and reverence, and that their
> home be their first school and their first Church. . . . Fathers
> and mothers should set their children a good example, taking
> them to Mass, vespers and sermons on Sundays and saints'
> days as often as possible. They should be punished as often as
> they neglect to do this.[67]

Another popular booklet, a catechism titled *Christen-Spiegel* (Christian Mirror), written in low German dialect by Diedrich Coelde, and
published in 1470 outlined the duties of parents in preventing children's
tendencies towards sin and evil:

> Children should be sent betimes to school, to worthy teachers,
> in order that they might be taught godly fear and reverence,
> and be saved from learning sin and evil in the streets. Those
> parents are to blame who object to the just punishment of
> their children.[68]

Sebastian Brant, whose *Narrenschiff* (Ship of Fools) was, next to the
Bible, the century's best seller, shares the view that only education can
save children from the follies of human excess and depravity:

> When children are not sent to school under the care of good
> schoolmasters they grow up to be wicked blasphemers, gam-
> blers and drunkards; for the beginning, the middle, and the
> end of a good life is a good education.[69]

Assuming the inheritance of sin to be the existential foundation
of a worldly existence, theoretically precluded the possibility of pure
childish innocence and attributed to children the natural inclination to
disobey, to resist and reject authority, and to doubt and misinterpret
God's laws. From infancy on, then, children had to be made cognizant
of their own sinful nature. The consequences of sin — punishment by
temporal authority, or punishment through eternal damnation by the
final divine authority — constituted the ultimate discipline and most effective method of control. For the very young, at least, threats and vi-
sions of "burning in eternal hell" undoubtedly instilled enough fear in
them to do as told. And as children enter their seventh year and, cor-
respondingly, have developed "real thoughts," the controlled conditions of schooling would intervene to help guard the young from the
mature, self-conscious and intentional forms of corruption.

The earlier that children were sent to school, the better; for as Luther had noted, reliance on parental guidance and discipline had proven largely unsuccessful:

> In the first place, there are some [parents] who are so lacking in piety and uprightness that they would not do it [instruction] if they could. . . . In the second place, the majority of parents are unqualified for it, and do not understand how children should be brought up and taught. . . . In the third place, even if parents were qualified and willing to do it themselves, yet on account of other employments and household duties they have not time for it, so that necessity requires us to have teachers for public schools.[70]

Luther disqualifies parents as reliable teachers of the young on moral and economic grounds, lacking piety and understanding, and constrained by the demands of labor at work and in the household. The need for public schools is justified as an almost natural economic and spiritual necessity for the good of children and parents, as well as for the general good.

Yet the very need to call upon and remind parents, mayors, and aldermen of their duty to provide a Christian education for the young, Luther considers in itself sinful;

> It is indeed a sin and shame that we must be aroused and incited to the duty of educating our children and of considering their higher interests, whereas nature itself should move us thereto.[71]

And so, public and compulsory schooling for all children under the guidance of "an industrious, pious school-master or teacher, who faithfully trains and educates," is seen by Luther as the only alternative to the inevitable sin and corruption which results from no schooling at all, or from schooling under the old, unreformed system.[72]

The position of the school master, a civil servant and servant of God, is elevated to new heights:

> Therefore let it be considered one of the highest virtues on earth faithfully to train the children of others, which duty but very few parents attend to themselves.[73]

Luther's recognition of and emphasis on the value of a state sponsored educational system increased the school master's social and spiritual prestige. The teachers' responsibility to community and God was enhanced and made concrete by the institutionalization of their training and their labor: state control of more formal and intensive teacher training programs in cloister schools, implementation of examinations and teacher certification, regular supervision of practicing teachers by district visitations, and work contracts stipulating tenure, salary, and housing.[74] School ordinances dictated curriculum, teaching methods, and school rules for students and teachers. Students were expected to adhere to codes of conduct much as teachers were expected to enforce the dictates of the ordinance. The distribution of printed ordinances to all schools within a given territory could, in principle, promote a uniform education; the continuation of regular church-school visitations provided extra, personalized insurance against deviation from the standards set down in the documents of the ordinances.

To promote social order and discipline, obedience to authority was an educational, secular and spiritual imperative. Habits of obedience drilled into children at home and at school were no different in kind from the obedience expected of teachers to school supervisors, inspectors and ordinances, or the submission and obedience demanded of the individual by God's word and will. Lutheran pedagogues, in Stone's estimation,

> approached their task with a set of values and presuppositions which ensured that the methods would be authoritarian and the objectives repressive. They hoped by such means to create a virtuous and holy society—and inevitably they failed.[75]

The accreditation of teaching coupled with the establishment of teacher training programs, examinations, and the issuance of teaching contracts can be seen as an early attempt at professionalization. Teachers, like students were to be fixed in writing through the documentation in personal portfolios of their educational record. This organization of individuals in the ledger and file systems of state administered school districts heralded the advent of bureaucratic school administration.

Professionalizing teaching and bureaucratizing schooling in conjunction with legislation that enforced mandatory school attendance, formalized both the educational discourse and the practices within which that discourse was embedded, and granted legitimacy to a new set of bureaucratic functionaries from the humble school master to senior visitation officials. These men—in Foucault's terms, "authorities of delimitation"—implemented the new pedagogy according to text that outlined every minute detail of the process and organization of teaching and learning; men in identical positions in other locations within a given region were teaching and supervising learning according to the same text. Visitation officials, also acting according to one text — *The Instructions* — were to ensure that uniformity and conformity characterized the new pedagogical endeavour, and that all centrally issued instructions were carried out "to the letter."

Chapter 5 examines in detail the implications of the administrative discourse as it emerged as part of the insitutionalizaton of early sixteenth century schooling. Suffice it for now to suggest that the burgeoning volume of print and institutional practices focused on and surrounding children during the early decades of sixteenth century Reformation Germany attest, at the least, to a manifest presence, not absence, of a concept of childhood. And although most of this official pedagogic discourse focused on the training of children at school, popular literature, as we have seen, and many of Luther's oral and printed sermons urged parents to do their part in the upbringing of the young.

Systematic record keeping under state control — since church administration had long lost credibility with the reformers — seemed the only viable means by which to organize the massive and complex undertaking of establishing their social and educational reform program. As Strauss notes,

> shaken by the sheer enormousness of the job of re-education they were taking on, the reformers came to realize . . . that they would be able to accomplish their objectives only by employing the legal authority and power of compulsion wielded by the state . . . to a significant extent the survival of the Reformation was becoming an administrative problem and a bureaucratic responsibility.[76]

Pedagogy for Home and School

In *Duties of Parents in Training Children* written in 1519, Luther advised against severe punishment and against the lack of discipline. Quoting Saint Paul: "Ye fathers, provoke not your children to wrath," Luther writes:

> under such an evil discipline, their disposition while yet tender and impressible, becomes partly clouded with fear and diffidence . . . a child, who has become timid, sullen and dejected

> in spirit, loses all his self-reliance. . . . For if children are ac-
> customed to tremble at every word spoken by their father or
> mother, they will start to quake forever after, even at the
> rustling of a leaf.[77]

The psychological insights expressed in this sermon about the consequences of intimidation and punishment of young children reveal a
sensitivity not dissimilar to the barber-surgeon Würtz's comments on
the effects on infants of coarse blankets and bedding. Luther continues, advising parents not to frighten children at night time, that
parents should not intimidate children to become cowardly or fearful,
but to instill in them a "wholesome fear" — that is, a fear of God and
parents alike. For if children fear only their parents, they are more
likely

> to fear the opinions of men, and so will become vacillating
> and cowardly. On this account children should be educated
> not only to fear their parents, but to feel that God will be
> angry with them if they do *not* fear their parents.[78]

In other words, children should be compelled to anticipate God's
wrath, and doubly so, if they do not also fear their parents. Luther admits that "far more can be accomplished by love, than by slavish fear
and constraint," but he reminds parents that it is the "duty of children
to learn the fear of God first of all," that "correction . . . saves the
soul of the child from the endless punishment of hell," and, therefore,
"let not the father spare the rod."[79]

The parent who neglects to raise children in the fear of God, a
duty which in itself is an honor to God, in effect, "hates children and
household," and "walks in darkness."[80] In Luther's words:

> For parents, who love their children blindly, and leave them
> to their own course, do no better in the end than if they hated
> them.[81]

Somewhere between "unbending severity" and "foolish fondness"
parents are to find the "middle ground" by which to instill in children
both fear and love of God, and of parents. Failure at successful
parenting is tantamount to hate of one's own children and sinful in the
eyes of God; children's failure to love — that is, to obey and respect —
and fear God and parents is sinful disobedience to the fourth commandment. The source of wickedness in children lies as much in their

inherited nature as it is a product of faulty childrearing—too much leniency or too much discipline. Parents, likewise, are in a "no win" situation. First, the toils of labor and household management prevent parents from attending to the systematic upbringing and moral instruction of the young; second, not having had the kind of education Luther envisioned for future generations, parents lack the necessary piety and understanding of childrearing; third, parents are guilty of either undue severity or "foolish fondness," and both attitudes equate with neglect and hate of children. Finally, the very issue of compelling parents to send their children to school is in itself "shameful" and "a sin." Luther never ceased to encourage parents to raise their young with a firm yet loving hand; on the whole, however, he seems to have mistrusted parents to carry out such a delicate and important task since most parents themselves did not have the kind of theologically correct and emotionally secure upbringing that he advocated.

Luther and Melanchthon had "hoped that schoolmasters would remedy this evil—that in school, at least, children would learn something good, and there have the fear of God implanted in their hearts."[82] But since schools and universities stood empty, "this hope, too, has come to nought."[83] And so, in the late 1520s and 1530s there emerged in the newly written and published school ordinances a new program of teaching and learning, a very specific concept of childhood. The newly designed curricula and instructional methods, the organization of learners according to ability and age, the building of new schools and the reorganization of old schools, the revised status of teachers, the implementation of examination and certification, and so forth, all derived from Luther's matured doctrinal fundamentalism.

Printing enabled the formalization and mass dissemination of this emergent concept of childhood in the form of official school documents, and in the popular pamphlet literature written for study at home. In addition, the visitation data which confirmed the disintegration of home, church and school, and, finally, the influence of Melanchthon who wrote the Lutheran program of study, contributed to the formation of a distinctly Protestant concept of childhood and youth.

5

Lutheran Pedagogical Practices

THE implementation of Luther's standardized curriculum – authored primarily by Melanchthon – required the parallel development of an administrative code; that is, the seminal attempt to prescribe and access a centralized curriculum gave rise to a formalized discourse on school administration. Hence, the early Lutheran stress on the mass transmission of literacy generated a prototypical bureaucratic discourse on teaching and learning in the context of state administered institutions of learning. Examination, certification and regular school visitations were intended to provide order within and among schools, and among teachers and learners – the beginnings of educational bureaucratization administered by the state. Secular and centralized administration of public schooling, so Luther and his contemporaries had hoped, would help reunite a religiously, politically, and socially disunified nation. Future generations, he believed, would acquire both the skills of literacy and the ideology of the new faith through enforced public schooling. As Luther envisioned the reformed social order, the governance of a new German state, independent of the religious-political domination of papal Italy, would require a moral and intellectual rebuilding of the populace from the ground up. And what better way to embark on a program of social and spiritual renewal but to lay the foundation in children and youth?

The causes and results of the 1525 Peasant Revolt had led Luther to become distrustful of vernacular schooling. Yet some thirty years later, at mid-century, the recognition of vernacular schools as essential and legitimate schools for the less intellectually able, the poor or the rural, reflected a renewed concern to bring territorial subjects under centralized state control by imbuing all subjects with a standard set of religious, social, and moral values. Underlying the emphasis on uniformity and repetition both in lesson scheduling and curricular content was a tacit recognition of the need for greater social discipline and civic order. And one important lesson that Luther did learn from the peasant uprising was that disciplinary efforts had to be more narrowly focused on youth since adults could not be trusted to act in the best interests of the social good. The ignorance of an unschooled peasantry, the ignorance of school children and teachers as revealed by the visitation documents, and the very serious threat of religious subversion from increasingly popular and vocal sectarian groups combined to force "Luther's shift in attention to shaping the young, as opposed to his earlier focus on all members of the community."[1] For it was

> the spectacle of [unschooled] peasants justifying their rebellion of 1525 by misrepresenting (in Luther's eyes) his religious message [which] turned the Great Reformer against any fostering of unsupervised book learning.[2]

In an era wracked by political strife over religious controversy, the surest way to preclude heterodoxy was to ensure religious conformity. The rising Anabaptist and other sectarian movements confirmed the fears of civil authorities and Reformation leaders alike that organized religiously motivated dissent was a realistic possibility. Hence, a lawful and centrally controlled indoctrination program, as Strauss puts it, designed to reach both poor and rural subjects was seen as one way to preclude the formation of sectarian splinter groups.[3]

The emphasis on the need for order, both civic and religious, is understandable in light of the kind of disarray documented by visitation examiners. And, in order to enforce uniformity of thought and behavior, clarity and simplicity of instruction, not only for children but also in the instructions to teachers themselves, was the key to inhibit any possibility of misinterpretation. The necessity for order, uniformity, and regularity is a recurring, explicit and overarching rule in all the school ordinances — the German word *Ordnung* (ordinance) means order and orderliness.

The Latin School

In order to appreciate how very serious the reformers saw their task of enforcing uniformity, coherence, and order within and among schools regionally scattered, the curricula for various types of schools and different age-grade levels warrant some scrutiny. For it was the attempt at mass implementation of these curricula that seemed to the reformers to require an administrative labor force and bureaucratic rule system to ensure orderly and uniform adherence by school masters to educational content and pedagogical practices. We turn first, then, to a brief examination of curricula for Latin, vernacular, and girls' schools before examining the administration of teaching and learning — the institutionalization of teachers and students.

Based on the model of a small Latin preparatory school Melanchthon had set up in his own home over a period of ten years, the main purpose of "elementary" schooling for boys was "to be the inculcation of true religion and sound learning."[4] Melanchthon's Latin school model was implemented as a state system throughout Saxony in 1528. Other territories implemented variations on his basic curricular and instructional outline throughout the century.

The first class, "Classis Elementariorum," was designed for boys with no prior reading or writing skills, and aimed at teaching the alphabet and the rudiments of Latin by use of the vernacular. Memorizing and reciting lists of Latin words and sentences was meant to expand the vocabulary as quickly as possible.[5] One hour daily was to be reserved for music and singing in which the whole class participated;[6]

> Religion was taught in Latin and learned by heart. Singing in Latin by the entire group formed a most important part of the daily program.[7]

Sundays were to be reserved for the exclusive study of the gospel; the schoolmaster gave scriptural expositions to the entire school and students were to recite assigned portions of the Bible as well as the

Lord's Prayer, the Apostle's Creed, and the Ten Commandments.[8] Provisions for study on Sundays specifically refer to Latin schools where students were full-time residents and not day students.

An elementary Latin grammar, written by Melanchthon in 1524, and printed in more than fifty editions that were still in use in all public schools in Saxony until the eighteenth century,[9] was used to teach "short sentences, prayers, pslams, etc., in Latin and in German."[10] From *Aesop's Fables*, which Luther "valued . . . very highly."[11] dialogues were selected which students memorized; this formed the basics for beginners' Latin conversation. Memorization of sentence structure and vocabulary preceded formal grammar study which, in Melanchthon's view, allowed students to become functional speakers of Latin first, and accomplished grammarians not until the second class. The textbook of the *Fables* was a version revised by Luther of a translation undertaken by German scholar Steinhöwel in the late 1400s, and consisted of a Latin and German version on each page.[12] Both Melanchthon and Luther believed in the use of literary works, instead of grammar texts for second language teaching. Reading in the sixteenth century meant oral reading which reflected the continuing influence of an oral, non-print tradition.[13] By reading literature for language study, conversational fluency was made orally explicit and conversational Latin could more readily be learned than by study of grammar texts. As Luther saw it,

> letters are dead words; the utterances of the mouth are living words, which in writing can never stand forth so distinct and so excellent.[14]

Language instruction and learning were to proceed from conversational fluency to a study of grammar. Latin, the "sacred tongue," "amiable" Greek, and "majestic" Hebrew,

> are much better learned by use and wont, than from these rules. . . . Is it not extremely absurd, for one who would learn the sacred tongue . . . to pick the language out of grammar alone?[15]

In the second class, to which a boy should not be transferred until the "master perceived that he was ripe for a more rigorous type of instruction,"[16] the use of German in classroom instruction was minimized, the study of Latin syntax was introduced, and readings included Terence and Vergil.[17] Upon entering the third class, the student was expected to be prepared to study the rudiments of logic and the principles of rhetoric, both considered to be indispensable skills for future university studies and eventual work in the professions. Conversational and written expertise in Latin was "required at a high standard of excellence"; readings include Livy, Horace, Ovid, and Cicero. Boys were grouped according to ability and those most advanced in their studies were taught Greek which Melanchthon, professor of Greek and theology at Wittenberg University, held in high esteem; some were encouraged to study Hebrew. Small group and individual instruction seemed to have been the norm for study of the languages, except "twice a week there shall be two lessons (e.g., upon a play of Plautus, or a book of Cicero's *Letters*) given to the entire class."[18]

The organization of subject matter, instruction, and learning followed a precise and clearly laid out format; since the Latin school was the training ground for future state and church leaders, the early preparation of the future ruling elite could not be left open to unmonitored, haphazard interpretation by individual teachers. The Latin schools came under particularly close scrutiny by the visitations.

The Vernacular School

Under the direction of Duke Christopher of Württemberg, the school ordinance of 1559 established a system of schools based on Melanchthon's three-tiered model of the Latin schools, but included vernacular schools, schools for the poor, and schools for girls. The object of schooling was:

> to carry youth from the elements through successive grades to the degree of culture demanded for offices in the church and in the state.[19]

The Württemberg school system benefited from thirty years of experience and data gathered by other territories in the establishment of compulsory and universal schooling. "Particular" or elementary schools were set up throughout districts from which students would progress to one of two "*pedagogia*" in either urban Stuttgart or Tübingen. Pedagogia were similar in kind to the modern high school, organized into five classes in preparation for university entrance.[20] "Lower" and "higher" cloister schools were residence schools which were designed primarily for the training of pastors, teachers, and parish administrators. Elementary schools were retained in larger towns; rural hamlets and villages provided basic catechical instruction throughout the parish. Under the article "Of the Instruction," the ordinance prescribes in concise, unambiguous terms what should be taught, how to teach, and how to classify and group learners. In the first class,

> those are placed who are first beginning to learn the alphabet; the second, those who are just beginning to read and write.[21]

Within each class, students are to be grouped according to ability,

> so that those of equal aptness to learn in each group may be put together, in order that the children may be stimulated to industry and the work of the schoolmaster may be lessened.[22]

Schoolmasters are advised not to "hurry the children" or promote them until competence is achieved. The teaching of the alphabet should follow a systematic approach, but occasionally the letters "should be broken up and with the letters mixed up the child should be asked to name some of the letters indiscriminately."[23]

While ability grouping may very well stimulate children to industry, it certainly would lessen the work of the schoolmaster. This early form of streaming, not unlike today's practices, undoubtedly facilitated more "efficient" instruction, testing, and classification. And since school achievement — classified according to ability — was to be certified through formal examinations, the move towards more efficient administration of the teaching and learning process laid the foundations for the classification of or, in Foucault's terms, the construction of the (certified) literate subject.

Once identification of letters is mastered, pronunciation of syllables follows; clarity of diction is stressed and "they shall be taught not to mumble the last syllables."[24] Following the ability to read "tolerably well," writing instruction begins for which children must have their own "special booklets." These the schoolmaster should examine regularly "having regard to defects in the form of the letters, the joining and adjustment thereof." Teachers are advised that "each child be kindly spoken to in a low tone and shown in a friendly way how each defect should be corrected."[25] Such a moderate approach is to ensure that "the children before all things shall be brought to the fear of God."[26] "Scandalous, shameful, sectarian books" are prohibited; authorized texts are the "Catechism, the Book of Psalms, the Proverbs of Solomon, Jesus Sirach, the New Testament, and the like."[27] The Catechism, as Luther had envisioned, was to be used as the basic text for language and moral instruction. One day a week at "one particular hour of the same day" was to be set aside for catechetical instruction;

> thus uniformity may be preserved, be drilled into the children, . . . that they become familiar with it, so that they will memorize it, practice it, and rightly understand and comprehend it.[28]

Uniformity of subject matter obviously was not enough; but "drilling" lessons into children at precise hours on specified days during each week might accomplish an exacting uniformity of thought and behavior. Uniform learning was best achieved by memorization, recitation, "simple instruction," and explanation "in a way that they can understand"; as well, competition was seen as another useful instructional method and motivational device whereby all the children in the school "shall compete in asking and answering questions about the Catechism."[29]

Music and singing instruction on certain days of the week at the same hour each day was to accustom children to singing in church and at school. Luther considered music and gymnastics an important part of the curriculum; he took a personal interest in the implementation of these programs in the schools around Wittenberg. In the 1528 ordinance, written by Luther's friend and colleague Johann Bugenhagen for the town of Brunswick, the teaching of vernacular and Latin songs is stressed:

> It is their [the choristers'] particular duty to teach all children, large and small, learned and ignorant, to sing (as Philip Melanchthon has stated in the aforementioned book) common songs in German and Latin. . . . In this way all children and youth shall learn to sing in the school.[30]

Singing collectively, but more importantly exercise in unison, constituted another, more ascetic regularity, disciplinary control and order. Foucault suggests that,

> exercise is that technique by which one imposes on the body tasks that are both repetitive and different, but always graduated. . . . exercise makes possible a perpetual characterization of the individual either in relation to this term, in relation to other individuals, or in relation to a type of itinerary.[31]

The itinerary to salvation and the itinerary of a pupil's school career were one and the same trajectory; moreover "it [exercise] thus assures, in the form of continuity and constraint, a growth, an observation, a qualification."[32] Singing and gymnastics were a means of ordering students' nonacademic time, of training impulsive young bodies into docility and habits of physical self-discipline, and of invoking a regimented ascetism and spiritualism reminiscent of the repetitive and graduated physical deprivations and ritual recitations of a monastic life. As Foucault notes:

> The theme of a perfection towards which the exemplary master guides the pupil became an authoritarian perfection of the pupils by the teacher; the ever-increasing rigorous exercises that the ascetic life proposed became tasks of increasing complexity that marked the gradual acquisition of knowledge and good behavious; the striving of the whole community towards salvation became the connective, permanent competition of individuals being classified in relation to one another. . . . In its mystical or ascetic form, exercise was a way of ordering earthly time for the conquest of salvation.[33]

The pursuit of faith on the path to salvation demanded, beyond the cognitive training in print literacy, a rigorous and orderly physical training; both mind and body must be well-disciplined and "correctly" used and "nothing must remain idle or useless."[34] A disciplined mind in a disciplined body was obviously very important for Luther.

Precise and detailed specification of all aspects of teaching and learning in both Latin and vernacular schools reflected new conceptions of discipline and pedagogy. Luther's incessant appeal between the 1520s and 1540s for more extensive popular schooling, and for the formal education of a new class of future state officials, were finally realized during mid-century. As the ordinances and visitation documents indicate, public school systems were operational by mid-century throughout reformed German territories.[35] The 1599 Württemberg ordinance examplifies the beginnings of modern school organization, the irrevocable trend towards a "totalized administration" of knowledge, and of children.[36] Regularity and repetition to promote conformity of thought and behavior was the new pedagogical method and aim; all school procedures were recorded, and all documents processed by state appointed officials. The increasingly efficient administration of schools and of pupil progress was catalogued and permanently fixed in the state archive, constituting a personal yet public record of a newly classified individual characterized by skills achievement, personal demeanor, examination records, and academic placement in relation to peers. The personal archive enabled the administrative grouping of individuals according to intellectual, behavioral, and social criteria. Yet students were grouped not only on paper: they were grouped physically and spatially in classrooms and schools in the same rank orders as their index cards were ordered in the administrator's bureau. The power of "dividing practices"—the classification and hierarchization of the examination—was based on and derived from the objectification of knowledge. The transmission, acquisition, and reproduction of school knowledge on the (confessional) examination comprised a procedural discourse within which the subject was constituted as an object of knowledge: in terms of the student as discursive object of study and scrutiny, and the student as embodiment of certifiable knowledge. The mandatory examination as part of compulsory schooling, Foucault comments, "is the technique by which power . . . holds them [school children] in a mechanism of objectification."[37] The school's discursive practices took children from a previously undifferentiated social mass and constructed them as objectified subjects by way of

> efficient and diverse applications of these combined procedures of power and knowledge . . . modes of classification, control and containment . . . to dominated groups or to groups formed and given an identity through the dividing practices.[38]

Schooling practices, then, aimed at reform of the individual and of society, generated administrative processes of grouping and individualizing human subjects and gave rise to inquisitorial processes of probing, questioning, observing, and examining. Such practices, however, were confined not solely to the disciplinary and social control of subjects but extended its surveillance network—the gaze—to include the institutions in which subjects were incarcerated for reform: the school as the site for reform of the mis- or unschooled individual. Personal inspection of the schools continued, as the Württemberg ordinance states:

> [the inspector shall] either alone, or, if necessary, with the bailiff and regular inspectors, visit the school at least once a month, and see how, and to what extent, these school-regulations of ours are carried out.[39]

Prescribing monthly school inspections rather than, say, annual or semiannual visitations which, today at any rate, would appear as more pragmatic and realistic, betrays a sense of urgency and seriousness among the school reformers intent on ensuring uniform, consistent and continued adherence to school regulations. School inspectors and their visitation documents were not beyond supervision either: "the highest body within the church administration annually reviewed the inspectors' reports and took action whenever needed."[40] Visitation officials were to be present not only at students' examinations and promotions, but were periodically required to examine the teachers as well. As W. Leonard comments,

> It is apparent that the schoolmaster is no longer master within his own domain, but has become a public servant in a minutely regulated institution.[41]

All of Bugenhagen's ordinances, in use throughout northern Germany, specified requisite teacher qualification, exact credentials necessary, preliminary examinations to be passed, practica to undergo, final examinations and disputations to pass before official appointment to a rector or sub-rectorship.[42] The examination, then, situated not only students but teachers as well in a network of writing that located and fixed them "in a system of intense registration and . . . documentary accumulation."[43] At the level of the student, "the examination enabled the teacher, while transmitting his knowledge, to transform his pupils into a whole field of knowledge."[44] At the level of the teacher, the examination enabled school administrators to transform teachers and teaching into a field of knowledge. The precise and rigid organization of time, space, and bodies in the schools, coupled with the confessional procedures of the examination and punitive procedures of the examination and punitive procedures of classroom control combined to constitute the site of early modern pedagogy where the calculated — prescientific — deployment of disciplinary power and knowledge intersected. As Foucault comments:

> The examination in the school was a constant exchange of knowledge; it guaranteed the movement of knowledge from the teacher to the pupil, but it extracted from the pupil a knowledge destined and reserved for the teacher. The school became the place for the elaboration of pedagogy. And just as the procedure of the hospital examination made possible the epistemological "thaw" of medicine, the age of the "examining" school marked the beginnings of a pedagogy that functions as a science.[45]

Concerning the student, the humanistic tone in the ordinance's instructional guidelines was balanced by clearly laid out directions for administering penalties. The Latin school ordinance (1525) of Brunswick, for instance, prohibited corporal punishment for students over seventeen years; instead, punishment was commuted to fines. The Kursachen ordinance of 1580 prescribed this punishment scale: a first verbal warning and reprimand followed by taking meals on the ground, the withholding of food and drink, whipping, confinement in the school dungeon, and, as a final resort, the explusion of the student from the school.[46]

A graduated system of fines, deprivation, and (solitary) confinement is the pedagogic-disciplinary counterpart of a judicial penalty system: In a disciplinary regime punishment involves a double juridico-natural reference."[47] Children should not be hurried through their lessons, nor be promoted until they are ready for more rigorous instruction—learning is a natural process. Yet each stage of learning is relatively fixed and regulated, and punctuated by the examination that demarcates difference among learners and among learning stages. Learning is both natural at the level of aptitude and performance, yet is artificial at the level of circumscribing constraints that classify performance, segment learning stages, and invoke a judicial disciplinary regime in response to infractions. Foucault explains this "juridico-natural" doublet:

> The order that the disciplinary punishments must enforce is of a mixed nature: it is an "artificial" order, explicitly laid down by a law, a programme, a set of regulations. But it is also an order defined by natural and observable processes: the duration of an apprenticeship, the time taken to perform an exercise, the level of aptitude refer to a regularity that is also a rule.[48]

A multi-tiered system of discipline and surveillance—of the student, the teacher, the school—repositioned children (and teachers) in newly institutionalized discursive practices and redefined them in a new discourse. As Foucault has observed of the disciplinary function of the examination in the schools, the prisons, and the military:

> The procedures of examination were accompanied at the same time by a system of intense registration and of documentary accumulation. A "power of writing" was constituted as an essential part in the mechanism of discipline.[49]

The compulsory registration of children in schools at once both institutionally separated them from society, and yet they became a formal and public part of society; their status was subtly redefined from association with the private domain of the family to the public domain of the state.

On the Education of Girls

In 1520 Luther wrote:

> Above all, in schools of all kinds the chief and most common lesson should be in the Scriptures, and for young boys in the Gospel; and would to God each town had also a girls' school, in which girls might be taught the Gospel for an hour daily, either in German or Latin.[50]

Prior to the 1520s, education for girls in local or parish schools was not common, although the education of daughters of the nobility or mercantile class in convent schools had been in vogue for centuries. Four years later, in 1524, Luther again called upon parents to send their sons and daughters to school which, as he points out, would not interfere with the duties expected from children at home:

> Boys shall attend upon such schools as I have in view an hour or two a day, and none less; spend their time at home, or in learning some trade. . . . So, too, your little girls may easily find time to go to school an hour a day and yet do all their household duties.[51]

The 1526 school reform document for the Electorate of Hesse made provisions for the education of girls who "were to be given some proficiency in reading, writing, and needlework. Religious instruction was to consist of Psalms and selected scriptural passages."[52] This same document contains Luther's most straightforward explanation of what he considered the essential purpose of public education:

> It is sufficient reason for establishing the best possible schools for boys and girls that the State, for its own advantage, needs well educated men and women for the better government of land and people, and the proper upbringing of children in the home.[53]

Education was not seen as an end in itself, but as a means for individuals to be of effective service to state and church. Men were to govern in the home, community, and society; women were to administer the household. Effective household management was seen as an important function for Christian women. Luther's denouncement of nunneries and his stress on the social and spiritual importance of marriage and the family, repositioned women from the private, socially invisible enclave of the cloister cell to the private enclave of the household.

Fellow reformer Johann Bugenhagen contributed much to the advancement of girls' education. A very influential and public figure, Bugenhagen was a close friend and colleague of Luther and Melanchthon; Bugenhagen held the chair of theology at Wittenberg University and was appointed pastor of the town church. His aim for educational reform was to combine both Latin and vernacular schools under one system. He wrote school ordinances for the cities of Hamburg (1529), Lübeck (1531), Bremen (1534), Pomerania (1535), Schleswig-Holstein (1542), Brunswick-Wolfenbüttel (1534), and for cities in Denmark and Norway during the late 1540s and early 1550s.[54] The aims and methods of his interpretation of Lutheran pedagogy, then, had widespread influence across northern Germany and parts of Scandinavia; according to Eby, "his services to popular education were greater in practical results than those of either Luther or Melanchthon."[55] From "Concerning the Girls' Schools" in the 1529 Brunswick ordinance, we can derive some specific ideas held by the author about how and what girls should be taught; and we can assume these educational practices to have been in general use given the wide distribution of Bugenhagen's ordinances.

In order that girls not be required to "go a great distance from their parents," it is suggested that "four schools for girls be held in four well selected parts of the city."[56] Girls are required to attend school daily, but "only one or at most two hours per day." In reference to payment of school fees to be paid to the school mistress "every quarter," it is pointed out that although "teaching involves trouble and labor," nonetheless, the teaching of girls requires only "a short time" — that is, girls can learn all that is deemed necessary "in a year or at most two years";

> for the girls need only to read, . . . to hear some exposition
> of the ten commandments, the creed and the Lords' Prayer,
> . . . what baptism is, . . . to learn to recite some passage
> from the New Testament . . . and some sacred history or

story suitable to girls, in order to exercise their memories . . .
and in addition to learn Christian song.[57]

Girls' formal education, then, is predominantly religious training, excluding study of the classics altogether. Subsequent to attending school for an hour or two, girls are to spend the rest of the day at home repeating their lessons, "and also to help their parents to keep house, and to observe, etc."[58]

Rudimentary literacy is essential for the Christian girl and future housewife who can best manage household and children if her thoughts and actions are grounded in an understanding of the words of God:

> From such girls who have laid hold of God's word there will
> come useful, skillful, happy, friendly, obedient, God-fearing,
> not superstitious, and self-willed housewives, who can control
> their servants, and train their children in obedience and
> respect them to reverence God.[59]

The ideal Christian woman, whether rich or poor, rural or urban, is here constructed as the mistress of the house—happy and obedient, self-willed yet God-fearing.

Poor or rich, parents should strive to have their daughters acquire a basic Christian education in the schools; poverty must not deter parents from sending their daughters to school for "if any burgher is very poor," there is a "general treasury for the poor" from which to draw school fees. In the 1529 Hamburg ordinance, Bugenhagen made a similar provision for a general treasury to fund rural schools for girls: "In every district a girls' school must be held."[60] Girls' schools under Bugenhagen's system were geographically separate from boys' schools. In contrast, the Württemberg ordinance of 1559 suggests that boys and girls were taught in the same school, if not in the same classroom, as the following directions to schoolmasters indicate: boys and "little girls" are to be "separately placed and taught"; the schoolmaster must "by no means allow them to run back and forth among each other, or to have disorderly relations with each other or to slip together."[61] Allowing boys and girls "to have disorderly relations with each other" just might encourage the kind of mayhem seen as inevitable when "weeds" mix with "good crops."

In theory and in practice boys' and girls' education was to be separate and different. Yet provision was made for a very basic education for girls which, although it emphasized traditional subject matter considered suitable for girls, aimed to teach girls rudimentary reading and writing skills. The mass promotion of literacy, irrespective of its essentially religious purposes, did give girls—particularly those in rural areas or from less affluent families—an opportunity to acquire the skills of reading and writing.

Undoubtedly, for many girls the opportunity to attend school was constrained by social or economic circumstances. Generations of girls continued to be raised at home unaffected by literacy or formal schooling. Given the greater availability and importance placed on boys' education, we can assume that in most communities more male than female household members could at least read. In practice, one literate person among two or three families would be sufficient to conduct Bible readings and discussions. And since the kind of vocations and professions that required a proficient literacy were only open to and held by men, the need to acquire a formal education or even basic literacy was decidedly less important for girls. Nonetheless, the Protestant reformers did provide the impetus for contemporary and succeeding educational reformers to include girls in the formal educational discourse and to create a place for them in the public school system.

School Administration

The teaching of literacy at the classroom level, once consolidated and institutionalized as part of the state apparatus, generated an educational administrative discourse. This institutional discourse necessitated concepts, language, procedures, and forms of documentation to express, in Foucault's words, "a technology of power."[62] What emerged were newly defined hierarchies of placement and advancement for student and teacher in schools; instruments, methods, techniques, and objectives for examinations and certification; curricula and instructional techniques to match students classified by age and ability; penalty systems for student or teacher infractions; notational and organizational systems for the administration of school and district finances, student enrollments, personal portfolios and so forth. In effect, a "bureaucratic" literacy emerged to administer the mass transmission of a "common" literacy.[63] The rise of a public school system in sixteenth century Protestant Germany, then, generated an official, state sanctioned discourse on pedagogy, and its bureaucratic administration.

This official educational discourse, borne of an initial "grass roots" literacy movement,[64] organized and rationalized the institu-

tional distribution of literacy and of literate subjects. The formalization of this discourse was reflected in the efforts made, as outlined in
the ordinances, to record and classify most aspects of students' and
teachers' institutional performance, and to centralize this information
as part of the state archive. On the school and community level, in
those states that adopted the Lutheran system of state education,
children, youths, and teachers were institutionalized and had become
identifiable, "visible" objects of knowledge through the written trace
left by their own writings, and by the notations made of them by their
supervisors and the surveillance experts of visitations. To regulate and
order the processes of learning and teaching required a system of
registration of all that went on in schools; detailed recordkeeping and
the wide distribution of school ordinances were meant "to regulate
everything."[65]

The Württemberg ordinance, for instance, explained to teachers
that "as we find heretofore in our schools a certain amount of diversity as regards teaching, authors and methods of teaching . . . which is
considered more of a hindrance than a help," the new ordinance "is
simply arranged and may have a childish appearance" which no school
master is likely to misinterpret.[66] Teachers are called upon to "regulate
everything" for the "good and advantage of the youth;" class and
school organization is based upon

> distinct division into classes, decurias, certain authors, hours,
> recitations and the like, according to which the preceptors are
> to regulate everything.[67]

Regulations in the preparatory *pedagogia* and cloister schools
were even more complex than in the Latin and "particular" schools.
Here the "maintenance of right order" was more elaborated and more
closely scrutinized; examinations and certification held a key role for
both students' and teachers' location, progression, and viability within
the institution. In Württemberg, for instance, teacher candidates
"were required to pass an examination testing their literacy, singing
ability, and knowledge of the catechism."[68] *Pedagogia* and cloister
schools were open only to boys, and the Württemberg ordinance called
upon parents to be "on the look out for boys . . . from twelve to
about fourteen years of age who have good minds and are desirous
and capable of higher studies."[69] The institutional regulations at
cloister schools and *pedagogia* indicate how thorough and detailed the
registration of students and teachers, learning and teaching had

become, and the kind of bureaucratic surveillance this imposed upon communities.

Admission to a *pedagogium* was dependent upon the results of both written and oral examinations. Prior to acceptance to examinations, a student was to present certificates from pastor and schoolmaster

> regarding his scholastic attainments, talents, and correct conduct . . . his age . . . demeanour, . . . the temporal means of his parents, and what sort of brothers and sisters he had, and whether these are educated or not, and, if so, to what extent in a Christian way.[70]

As well, parents or guardians were required to submit their written consent and, thereby, "obligate themselves" to support a boy's course of study. The school, then, served "not simply [to] train docile children," but also

> to supervise their parents, to gain information as to their way of life, their resources, their piety, their morals . . . to constitute minute social observatories that penetrate even to the adults and exercise regular supervision over them.[71]

A detailed report of each student's ability and family background was to be prepared by counsellors and kept on file in Stuttgart, territorial capital of Württemberg. Explaining the purpose of centralized documentation, the ordinance states:

> a regular record and catalogue should be in hand, so that at any time they [administrators] may see from it what sort of boys are in each cloister, and how many vacancies there are.[72]

It was hoped that the distribution of printed, identical ordinances and school texts to every school in a territory, electorate, or principality would standardize instructional practices and curricular interpretation. The data collected by periodic visitations, in addition to centralized documentation of examination results, students' personal portfolios, and school enrollment records, enabled closer and more far-reaching scrutiny of school affairs independent of personal monitoring. Under a system of state-administered schooling, the accumulation of personal files of students, their families, and schoolmasters provided an additional and alternative account of the population, supplementing the more traditional census data derived from municipal tax records.

Printing enabled the mass promotion of literacy through public education; the standardization of public schooling depended upon concerted efforts to enforce instructional, curricular, and administrative uniformity. The Württemberg ordinances and the attendant institutional processing of print and people, which the centralized administration of public schooling required, illustrate how the growth of an institution specializing in, among other things, the transmission, production and reproduction of knowledge, leads to the necessary correlative expansion of and refinement in methods of efficient administration.

Teaching and learning in public school, then, by mid-century had become a clearly defined system of graduated curricula and instruction related to age-grade levels. School administration – student and teacher recruitment, examinations, certification, school finances, the administration of different types of schools, and teacher training – had come under state jurisdiction, usually located in regional capitals. State and church affairs were not disjoined, but state legislation was superimposed on municipal and ecclesiastical affairs.

Public schooling had seemed to the reformers a pragmatic idea and necessary precondition to reunite a religiously, politically and socially disunified nation that recognized the need to liberate itself from the cultural, intellectual, and religious domination of papal Italy. A key issue for German national autonomy was the shift of religious-political power from Imperial Rome to domestic authority over local church and secular affairs.[73] The push for communities to select their own pastor who would, in turn, participate in the hiring of teachers, illustrates this trend towards local secular authority over religious and civil issues. The accumulation of data – about students, their families, and teachers, examinations, certifications, schools and school district finances, enrollment records, and so forth – was meant to improve the efficiency of school administration and to provide order within and among schools and communities. This accumulated knowledge, in turn, would be reapplied to the system from which the data was derived to further improve its growth, efficiency, or quality, all of which was an investment of sorts in the production of knowledge and skills embodied in children and youths. The "network of writing" or record-keeping by standardized and multiple printed copies of documents – the prescriptive ordinances and descriptive examinations – made possible the systematization of schooling and educational administration.

Institutionalized Mass Literacy, Surveillance, and Social Control

Printed text, as distinct from manuscript text, enabled literacy, in the context discussed here, to develop two forms. First, it promoted print literacy encoded primarily in religious text; at the object level of print literacy, then, the transmission of graphemic, syntactic and semantic elements of the German language were inseparable from the ideological messages embedded in popular literacy. Phonemic elements differed regionally since high and low German texts were published throughout the century. Importantly, the most widely acknowledged consequence of print technology and the subsequent spread of popular literacy (i.e., rudimentary reading skills and, to a lesser extent, writing skills) was its inextricable link with the spread of "popular religion."

The second consequence of the institutional promotion of literacy by the state through schools was the kind of administrative literacy that the rather complex organization of an unprecedented accumulation of documents engendered. At this second, or meta level of literacy, the school apparatus required interpretive, notational, and classificatory schemes with which to organize diverse information about a large number of people in and associated with a district's schools. The success or failure of a school could be judged according to school records and visitation documents that gave extensive and minute accounts of communities: schools, church, individuals, and families. And so, educational administrators and senior evaluators in charge of visitations became the instruments for the political supervision of collective forms of behavior, attitude, and performances through the rewriting of accumulated and interpreted data in reports, ministerial registers, and revised ordinances.

"The school," as Foucault notes, "became a sort of apparatus of uninterrupted examination that duplicated along its entire length the operation of teaching."[74] Foucault here describes the eighteenth century French school, but his observations apply aptly to the sixteenth century German school which was established and functioned with the same zeal for "regulat[ing] everything" as La Salle had prescribed for the French Christian Schools. The examination, perhaps more than the visitation documents of recorded observations, constituted and made visible the literate individual: at once both as individuated subject and as object of knowledge. "For a long time," prior to the establishment of compulsory schooling, "ordinary individuality—the everyday individuality of everybody—remained below the threshold of description."[75] The disciplinary apparatus of the school, and in particular the examination, "reversed this relation, lowered the threshold of describable individuality and made of this description a means of control and a method of domination."[76] By "transform[ing] the economy of visibility into the exercise of power,"[77] by "introduc[ing] individuality into the field of documentation,"[78] and by "mak[ing] each individual into a 'case',"[79] the examination became a disciplinary technology that constituted individuals as elements of power and knowledge.[80] In pursuit of building, from the ground up, a moral, educated, and disciplined citizenry, Luther's mass literacy campaign mobilized all possible forces of social registration which laid the foundation for the modern state apparatus. Registration of the individual on the grid of the social collective marked the foundational (disciplinary) principles that became embedded in the discourses of the human sciences—the pillars upon which the modern state rests in an uneasy sway.

Public schooling based on the Lutheran model took root because printing helped popularize the religiously grounded rationale for the duty of individuals to become proficient in reading and because literacy, for the most part, had been accepted as the key to true faith and possible salvation. Public schooling can be considered as both consequence and concomitant of a mass promoted ideology that stressed the importance of individual duties and right of access to the printed word. Knowledge was no longer to be the private domain of clerics but, under state control, was to become "public property," accessible to all. The official power, as vested in teaching and administrative posts, to select and transmit public knowledge, then, could be attained, in principle, by anyone since all children were legally compelled to attend public schools.

A half century after Luther had helped stir the German people to a social, political, and a kind of intellectual reawakening, education had itself become part of a social and political environment which, as Cressy notes of the development of education in England, provided a fairly well-defined and established context that would define the values, uses and criteria for literacy.[81] In this sense, education as a state institution and as a political and social structure did take over the role of defining and evaluating literacy, and of establishing certain criteria for specific literacy skills required of educational practitioners.[82] This historical development contrasts with the earlier push to promote literacy according to the criteria and aims set forth by Luther and contemporary educational reformers who had more narrowly defined literacy: First, to acquire the skills of reading to decipher and comprehend the scriptures; second, to acquire the Lutheran version of a "classical" education along the lines set out by Melanchthon to facilitate service to and leadership in the church and state. These early concerns about children and adolescents did, nonetheless, directly and indirectly bring the young under professional scrutiny.

Public schooling was not in effect throughout the German Empire. But in those states that did implement universal schooling, children's lives were affected. For many, learning had been removed from the home, the streets, or the community and had been replaced by an organized and regimented institutional setting where rewards, punishments, and the ideas and skills to be learned were provided by an authority other than the more familiar and personal authority of family and community members. Public schooling undoubtedly affected parents who were legally compelled to send their children to school, and who could no longer rely on the economic benefits of free help received from children's labor in the household or workplace. For most children a part of each day was spent in schools; for others public schooling provided access to more and advanced schooling — an extended and more comprehensive institutionalization of their lives and their learning.

As the state assumed greater authority and responsibility over the social order, the need to systematize and enforce public schooling, to encourage advanced study, and to institutionalize the young seemed to the reformers a reasonable and necessary step towards preparing future generations to perpetuate and uphold an ideology hard won in the face of internal and external political and religious adversity. And finally, from a more global historical perspective, the Lutheran establishment of public and compulsory schooling reflects two very radical and fundamental historical changes, the significance of which we can only appreciate in historical retrospect: the shift of authority over education from the church to the state, and the gradual transition from oral to print culture.

6

The Discursive
Formation of Childhood

THIS book has investigated the influence of printing and Protestantism on pedagogy in sixteenth century German society. In attempting to order diverse evidence and to demonstrate how a variety of relations converged to bring about a change in thought about the young, it has been impossible to dissociate the history of childhood from family and educational history, the advent of typography from the history of literacy, or to discuss the rise of Protestantism independent of its reliance on and encouragement of printing and literacy. My intent here has not been "to revive the ridiculous thesis that the Reformation was the child of the printing press."[1] However, the spread of Reformation ideas and the development of the Reformation as a social, political, and educational movement relied on the potential of mechanized printing and extended that potential. My contention has been that early Protestantism and the production and consumption of printed text were mutually reinforcing within the context of specific sociocultural, political, and economic conditions, and of the prevailing intellectual milieu of sixteenth century Germany.

As we have seen, central to Luther's campaign for religious and social reform was his skillful use of print technology and the systematic introduction of vernacular German in the public and academic discourse. The initial development of what was to become known as Protestantism was the result of Luther's rejection and revision of traditional theological concepts. The subsequent diffusion of his ideas was made possible by their mass dissemination in print and printed illustrations, as well as by the more traditional means of oral communication: the preachings of evangelists. Luther's words and ideas reached a public already well familiar with print; since the invention of the press in 1450, posters, placards, handbills, broadsheets, and so forth had been utilized widely to provide information to the public. Lutheran reformers made calculated use of print technology to publicize and generate public support for their movement. Before Luther became a figure of public and political interest in 1517, German burghers and peasants, artisans and merchants, and many humanist academics shared a feeling of unrest and dissatisfaction with existing social, economic, and political-religious conditions, and were ready for a change towards what for them promised to be a more just and Christian society. The economic conditions and political events preceding the 1525 Peasant Revolt and the subsequent consequences of the revolution on the course of the Reformation have been discussed to provide a broader context within which to situate the educational reform movement that began in the late 1520s.

Different points of connection in the relationship between the first century of printing and early Protestantism have been focused on in this study. Commonly unrelated historical data have been linked to the central theme—the history of the discourse on childhood—in an effort to establish the network of historically antecedent and contemporaneous relations that set the conditions for historical change in childreading, that is education practice and ideas. My initial premise was that the first century of transition from script to print culture generated, inter alia, a change in ideas about children from premodern to modern notions of childhood. The early shift from oral to print communications generated the formalization and systematization of language and of discourses; speech and ideas became fixed in print, visible to a mass audience. The Reformation, I have argued, was the first major social and ideological movement after the invention of moveable type that incorporated the printed word and print literacy as a fundamental constituent of its ideology, and that extensively used print to promote that ideology. The establishment of public schools reinforced the legitimacy of "book learning" which had already been popularized and sanctioned by Luther's vernacular translation of the Bible, and by his insistent call for a universal priesthood—a mass readership of the Bible. The redefinition of childhood under Protestantism had to do with book learning; in a circuitous way, Luther's text-centered religion of individualism, the establishment of schools, and the development of a public, as distinct from scholarly, pedagogic discourse, can be considered as one indirect consequence of the early shift from script to print. The displacement of church in favor of state authority over secular affairs, reflected in state administered public and compulsory schooling and in the public secular discourse that circumscribed institutionalized schooling, is a parallel development—an indirect consequence and indicator—of the shift from script to print.

Starting in the early sixteenth century, western Europe underwent a general transition from oral to print culture, from restricted to mass literacy. European society underwent this process of change under varying circumstances; different political, religious, or economic constraints encouraged printing and literacy in some countries, and inhibited them in others. Similarly, the spread of Protestantism was readily adopted by some countries and vehemently rejected in others according to varying regional political-religious loyalties and affiliations. The difference in attitude towards book learning between Catholic France and Protestant Germany illustrates the differential consequences of promoting or discouraging printing and literacy on ideas about education and family and childhood. As Eisenstein has demonstrated in detail, "going by the book" in secular and spiritual matters was far more important for Protestants than for Catholics.

At the beginning of the sixteenth century, the mass dissemination of conduct books, herbals, domestic guides and marriage manuals, health and "self-help" books was, in many ways, the mass distribution of old advice in a new medium. Yet by mid-century, old advice was mixed with the "reformed religion"—with new ideas about the family, the individual, different social and spiritual conduct, and the management of community affairs. Reflecting Luther's influence, more vernacular books concerned with secular and spiritual issues infiltrated Protestant households than Catholic ones. Along the same lines, self-help books on reading, writing, or elementary mathematics proliferated in Protestant households. Luther's emphasis on the necessity for individual literacy as the gateway to potential salvation and as indispensable for participation in secular "good works," underscored the fervor with which Protestants — and perhaps initially only the already educated urban burghers — pursued their own reeducation.

My premise has been that the advent of printing made possible the subsequent spread of ideas, literacy, and the diffusion of Lutheran ideology, a central part of which was a revised concept of the family and of childhood. In chapter 3, I discussed the expansion of printing prior to 1500; it was noted that at the turn of the century, "the book had arrived." The trend towards the use of the vernacular in scholarly, theological and secular works was well-established, and literacy can be assumed to have spread in relation to the geographical expansion of printing and the increased output of published works. Luther seized upon the availability and potential of print technology and further promoted printing and literacy in an effort to promote his own ideas via print.

The rise of Protestantism and the advent of printing were significant changes in themselves. When taken together in relation to those antecedent and contemporaneous forces — social, economic, technological, political, and cultural — that set favorable conditions for the Reformation to take hold, the fact that a demand for "schooling for print" would emerge is not surprising. Moreover, when examining those intellectual forerunners who informed Luther's views and who served as catalysts for his contestations with theological principles and practices, it becomes equally clear that schooling for print would become schooling for the new belief. Schooling for print and for the new faith would provide the rudimentary literacy skills that would enable the general public to have access to the cheap and simply written pamphlets of Luther's sermons, the Catechisms, song and prayer books that were meant to constitute ideological and social cohesion for family, community, and Protestant society.

Public schooling may have initially produced generations of readers competent only to read pamphlets, posters, or broadsheets. As well, the expense of books undoubtedly made them inaccessible to most common folk. And despite Luther's campaign to put a Bible in every household, there is no evidence to verify how many Bibles did, in fact, become a part of daily life; inventories of wills that list Bibles and other books tend to reflect book ownership among those affluent enough to register a will. In short, the beginnings of public schooling can be said to have arisen out of the need for mass ideological conversion, rather than for purely altruistic purposes.

In chapter 4, Luther's views were discussed principally in relation to Saint Augustine whose doctrine of sin and predestination Luther resurrected. Correct and systematic training by home and school was considered a logical and pragmatic solution to the potential manifestations of sin in children and youth. At a more fundamental level, underlying the shift in ideas about children was Luther's radical conception of the relationship between the individual and God. At the core of Luther's doctrinal polemic was his belief that the only source of religious truth was the divine word as originally set down in the scriptures. Salvation could be attained only by faith and not, for instance, through the purchase of indulgences. Moreover, faith could only be attained by the grace of God which, in turn, women and men could only have access to via scripture. The importance of the authority of the Biblical text and Luther's religious individualism would lead to the need for vernacular interpretations of the Bible in order to make God's word accessible to everyone; it would eventually lead to the need and demand for an educational system open to all children, one that would teach the skills of reading and writing while providing instruction in the new faith.

If, as Luther envisioned, there should be no difference between the spiritual estate (priesthood), and the temporal-secular estate (laity), but that all true Christians are, indeed, a priesthood of believers, then, in principle, all individuals have an equal duty and right to confront God's words as revealed in the divine text. The existence of the press that enabled the mass production of printed text, I would suggest, made possible the popular idea that there be a Bible in every household, that every household be transformed into a church, and every household member into a priest. Insofar as printing in the early decades of the sixteenth century was already an established craft and mode of communication, we might rightfully assume that Luther's call for a Bible in every household, which can be seen as the practical underpinning of "a priesthood of all believers," is a direct consequence of the printing press—multiple duplications of text were possible before Luther formulated his text-centered theology.

Similarly, the establishment of a public school system and the standardization of that system depended upon the mass production of school texts and school ordinances. Public schooling, as we have seen, was considered by Protestant reformers as a necessary precondition for socio-religious change; universal schooling would provide the means by which to inculcate children with Christian morals and values while teaching them to read and write. The reformers had hoped that by providing near universal access to a basic education, entire generations of children would attend school with the inevitable outcome that systematic and uniform molding of young minds would result in the eventual transition to a more just and Christian social order. It would be the responsibility of the graduates of the new educational system, trained in the new faith, to assume positions of power and leadership in the church and state and, thereby, consolidate and secure the reformed social order.

Books of the proper kind and book learning were the key to educating and enlightening both young and old. Prior to the sixteenth century, book learning had been the domain of "old men and monks," in Eisenstein's words. In sixteenth century Lutheran Germany, as in other Protestant regions throughout Europe, book learning "gradually became the focus of daily life during childhood, adolescence and early manhood."[2] Domestic manuals prescribed the new roles mothers and fathers were to assume in childrearing; state legislated school ordinances prescribed curricula and instructional methods for schoolmasters. Diversity in school instruction was frowned upon by the educational authorities. Standardized curricula, teacher and student examinations, school rules and punishment scales, teachers' guides, and so forth, were directives contained in the multiple printed and distributed school ordinances that were meant to eliminate diversity and promote uniformity of teaching and learning of standardized school knowledge. Systematic school inspections were aimed at bringing both the schoolmaster and the student — and by extension, the community — under more uniform and centralized control.

The establishment of different kinds of schools, the creation of textbooks designed to match age-grade related ability levels, and the implementation of a graduated examination and certification system reflect a heightened awareness of children's developmental stages and correlative cognitive abilities. Moreover, "dividing practices" such as the examination, the educational certificate, and curricula matched with ability levels, indicate the emergence of a sensibility that Foucault associates with the "classical era" which he characterizes as an era preoccupied with situating, naming, differentiating, and classifying objects on the taxonomic grids of visible, identifiable differences.[3] The establishment of a clearly articulated sequence of learning stages (i.e., curricula, classes, and schools) and the provision of printed materials and teachers trained to address distinct ability levels, marked the early foundations of modern schooling. Regularity, repetition, and regimentation became the ordering principle for the new pedagogy which, in turn, constituted the means for a new social discipline.

The most decisive and critical step undertaken by the educational reformers of the Reformation, and one not overlooked by educational historians, was the establishment of universal schooling, and the transfer of administrative power over education from the church to the state.

Children became a legalized object of state scrutiny; authority over children was no longer the sole domain of parents or legal guardians. Schooling added a new dimension to children's lives. Not only did learning become institutionalized and formalized—Eisenstein notes this transition as the shift from "learning by doing" to "learning by reading"—but, also, educational success or failure brought with it rewards and punishments meted out by institutional authorities, not household members. Moreover, success or failure at school began to imply eventual occupational status as the system of examination and certification became more pervasive and took on greater importance. We can assume that this new educational intervention did not affect all children; the inheritance of property or a commercial enterprise undoubtedly continued to set the occupational futures for many children, particularly for boys. Yet, public education and the availability of financial assistance for economically disadvantaged children did provide a legitimate means for those children whose families had neither property nor name to bequeath, to better their station in life by acquiring enough educational capital to become 'upwardly mobile.'

The Birth of the School: An Archeology of Childhood

The relationships among printing, literacy, Protestantism, and ideas about childhood are complex. However, although forces such as print, mass literacy, and the Reformation are both cause and consequence, the printing press did help the Reformation take root which, in turn, explicitly promoted literacy and an education for literacy. To recapitulate: I began this book questioning Aries' suggestion that concepts of the family and childhood changed in European society during the seventeenth and eighteenth centuries. Examining Stone's work on the English family, I found that similar characteristics of change in family life and structure, and childrearing practices emerged during the mid-sixteenth century. The differences between Protestant England and Catholic France with respect to family and educational history became apparent; the shift from premodern to early modern concepts of the family and childhood was not a uniform transition in European thought. Under English Protestantism changes in education, family relations and structure predated similar changes noted for seventeenth and eighteenth century France. Consequently, I sensed that the early developments of the Protestant Reformation warranted further investigation. My initial survey of sixteenth century German social history revealed obvious links between early print technology and the spread of Luther's ideas.

By examining the historical conditions that led to the development of an "official," formalized discourse on pedagogy via the implementation of public schooling in pro-Lutheran regions, I have attempted to specify a network of relationships that converged in an identifiable discourse on childhood and youth. This secular discourse marked the early modern shift in ideas about children which, as Aries puts it, reflected in "a revival at the beginning of modern times of an interest in education."[4] And while Aries situates this interest in education roughly during the eighteenth century, I have found an earlier interest in children and education located in the sixteenth century Protestant discourse on pedagogy. The sixteenth century Protestant educational revival I have found to be a consequence of the introduction of moveable type and certain tenets of Lutheranism which, in time, demanded and furthered literacy and its formalization: the standardization of vernacular German, the graphemic standardization of print, and the establishment of public schools. Underlying any discourse on schooling are necessarily concepts of teaching, learning, cognition, psychosocial development, and hence—the child. The historical evidence provided here points to a formalized and highly specified discourse on home and school pedagogy within which a concept of childhood was clearly articulated.

The changes in family life and ideas about childhood that Aries documents for the French family during the seventeenth and eighteenth centuries, and similar changes in the English family starting in the mid-sixteenth century as noted by Stone, when taken as a whole, can be interpreted as a reflection of rather broad historical change (in ideas, family structure, ecnomic organization, and so forth) during a rather broadly defined historical era—"early modern times." I suggest that the beginnings of these conceptual and practical changes concerning the family, childhood, and education can be traced to and dated by the events and literature of the German Protestant Reformation during the 1520s to 1560s.

If we accept Aries' suggestion that in premodern times children mingled freely with adult society and had more social freedoms, then the separation of children from that milieu by the schools and by parents whose duty it now became to impose more stringent controls on the young, supports Aries' contention that the early modern shift in ideas about children was characterized, in part, by a deprivation of social freedoms the young had previously enjoyed. The school and the family were reconceived as the primary "disciplinary sites" for the transmission of Christian morals and values based on notions of individual self-discipline. School and family exercised a newly justified authority and power over children. The school in particular emerged as the principal state apparatus by and within which the social body was regimented and trained into a social discipline based on individuating the subject within the social collective. Individual self-discipline was seen as prerequisite to greater social cohesion and discipline. Individual faith was considered the cornerstone of a collective "priesthood of believers" united as one church which, in turn, would form the backbone of a spirituality, socially, culturally, and politically unified nation. Childhood became the target upon which the rebuilding of a fragmented society from the ground up was focused.

Young children were no longer considered unimportant — their existence ceased to "not count." Instead, the young were seen as the unschooled, in need of moral guidance and protection from and control over their potentially deviant nature. But the ultimate aim of the new pedagogy that appears in retrospect to have been an authoritarian pedagogy of repression, was to provide long-term beneficial consequences for the individual and for society. To protect the young from what the reformers judged to be the overwhelming power of sin, mandatory schooling, close supervision, discipline, and years of reciting appropriate school (textual) knowledge were seen as the only viable correctives for the kind of moral decay that appeared to pervade society. As well, among the educated and emergent mercantile class there was an increasing recognition of the need for institutionally socialized, skilled, and literate workers. The recognition that the future of the state and church, community, and family was dependent upon the young, upon universal access to institutional facilities in which to train the young, and upon parents sending their children to school, when taken together, reflects an intent to promote greater (social) justice and (spiritual) equality.

As noted at the beginning, my purpose here has not been solely to refute Aries' claims, but to use his work as a point of contrast against which to note similar historical change in ideas about the family and childhood in a different society, at a different juncture in time. In recent years, the debate over his work has subsided and historians of the family and childhood have settled into their disciplinary niches to pursue their historical investigations from different methodological vantage points. Social history, and to a lesser extent psychohistory, are now at the disciplinary forefront exploring historical concepts of childhood and childrearing practices. This study has followed neither methodological course. Instead, by constructing a framework for analyzing the emergence and manifestation of a discourse as suggested by Foucault, it has been possible to move away from a linear, progressive account of historical change (narrative history), from less generalizable accounts of microhistorical studies (social history), from the human agent determinism of psychoanalytic and phylo/onto-genic perspectives (psychohistory), and from the limitations of quali-tative description derived from statistically-based studies (demo-graphic history).

By setting out a "discursive field," wherein the formal (written) discourse is not abstracted from its author(s) nor interpreted in terms of its author, where discourse and author are necessarily a product and intrinsic part of the practices formulated by that same discourse, and where discursive omission and silence are as critical a part of a dis-course as that which it includes, it is possible to write a history that can incorporate "great events" with personal records, one that links, say, technological innovation in one field with its social consequences in other spheres. Moreover, it enables the uncovering of discursive assump-tions that underlie a given set of practices (e.g., religious, disciplinary, pedagogic). Conversely, it allows the uncovering of unsuspected his-torically antecedent and concurrent practices, and intellectual points of connection that contribute to the formation and formalization of a discourse. In other words, an archeology of discourse is not confined to synchronic analysis but juxtaposes the historical present against the historical past in order to trace — geneologically — the emergence and dis-appearance, trajectories and transformations of concepts or dis-courses across time. In this sense and in contrast to other historical ap-proaches (e.g., social, psycho-, or narrative history) that undertake in-quiry on the basis of a priori operant principles — methodologically, and in terms of disciplinary-based concepts of the family, society, in-dividual, education and so forth — a history of discourse leaves enough conceptual room to allow a given set of concepts or ideas to emerge from within their own context. For example, and in specific reference to the history of childhood, a history of discourse does not investigate childrearing practices, or text for and about children with a priori def-initions of the child, the family or society that, for instance, anthropo-logically-based studies presuppose. A history of discourse presupposes a field of discourse — not only or necessarily text, but all historical in-scriptions in diverse forms such as architecture, relics, technology, roads or trade routes. Using Foucault's archeological approach to his-tory, we dig for clues and relics of knowledge at the discursive site. Yet, this immersion in context easily runs the risk of providing an ob-ject level analysis. What then, is the value of discursive history for the study of history in general, and specifically, for the history of childhood?

First, to address the former, historical descriptions are necessarily ordered by present concepts of history and current knowledge; in short, by the contemporary "episteme" of which this text and this very discussion of historical method is a part. Nonetheless, an archeological approach to history is an alternative to reproducing and reconfirming age-old static concepts of an overriding cultural unity or a central epistemological principle by which an historical period or society is said to cohere. Instead, the intent is to trace one history or series of histories by reordering historical traces: "books, texts, accounts, registers, acts, buildings, institutions, laws, techniques, objects, customs, etc."[5] Second, this repositioning of historical data—the juxtaposition of history's "material documentation" traditionally assumed to be unrelated and disparate—allows the historian to identify and isolate different sets of historical "objects." Such objects have their own history and structure, sets of practices, customs or laws, and contain their own conditions of possibility. An historical object such as the printing press, for instance, generated, inter alia, the possibility of mass producing printed text, established a new direction in the development of the paper industry, advanced the development and specialization of typesetting, engendered institutionalized book learning via mass schooling, and created a new culture industry whose agents were the new "printer-scholars."

By sorting out separate historical series, then, and tracing their possibilities, links to and overlaps with other discourses and practices —some unsuspected, others familiar—will emerge. The context within which social forms or ideas emerge, develop or disappear, can be established without reducing history to a myriad of individual discourses all relative to historically adjacent series, and without unifying an asymmetrical and complex history under the traditional "great moments in history" umbrella. A history of discourse is a mode of inquiry that allows the historican to map new, previously unconsidered trajectories, to develop a matrix or grid, as it were, within which to situate diverse historical data. In such a "constellation," reordered data will bear directly and/or indirectly on the discourse under study in ways—opposing, complementary, contradictory—that traditional histories have failed to note and conceptually have been unable to consider.

In this study some of these connections have surfaced: early Protestantism and the advent of printing were historically contemporaneous and complementary phenomena. Luther opposed church doctrine and practice and, in a link back with a former intellectual tradition, he retrieved and reformulated Augustinian doctrine. Luther's rise to prominence marks a unique historical juncture—at once both continuous and discontinuous—one which marked a most radical break with the immediate past while reinstating an intellectual continuity with an earlier past. The spiritual liberation of the individual was based on Luther's incorporation from the more distant past of an essentially negative concept of the individual and human nature. This concept of the individual formed the basis of a projected future—salvation by faith alone—of ostensible individual liberation, reform, secular and spiritual justice and equality, and relief from medieval oppression by church and landlord.

Foucault argues for an historical inquiry that does not seek to explain events, ideas, or innovation as part of the progressive unfolding of consciousness, as "simple causality" or "circular determination," but one that individualizes historical series, describes the relations between them, and distinguishes types of events at different levels. Accordingly, we can see that in the formation of the Lutheran discourse an individualist ethic emerged in opposition to the medieval collectivization of social and spiritual life. Yet, this individualism was seen as foundational to the future reestablishment of a cohesive social collective. And while this focus on individualism seemed, indeed, to mark a discontinuity with the immediate past, the fundamental tenets of the new faith formed the strongest existential and ideological links to and continuity with an intellectual past (i.e., Augustinian doctrine) from which the ideology that Luther opposed, originally emerged.

Looking to a different level and a different series across time, it becomes apparent that printing engendered analogous transformations in its materiality (the text) and immateriality (mode of thought and communication). The first fifty years of printing reproduced the texts of the past. The initial organization of language in print was the encoding of oral language in print; manuscript form and speech continued through the medium of print. The collectivizing force of information exchange in an oral culture was transformed by print into what is generally considered as the privatization of thought and language. Inasmuch as this privatization resembled the privatization of faith as set forth by Luther, so the standardization of language and thought in print, and the development of a mass readership confronting essentially the same few texts (i.e., the Bible, pamphlets, calendars, domestic manuals, etc.), recollectivized individual readers and believers.

We have, then, in the two series—printing and Protestantism—historical discontinuity yet continuity through transformation, succession and difference, overlap and interplay of conceptual and sociopractical similarities, disappearance on one level and repetition on another. And together through the systematization of language and ideas in print and, subsequently, the systematization of Lutheran ideology, a discourse emerged defining its own level of formalization and legitimacy. Underneath and contained within it, this primary theological discourse generated and was constituted by a "subseries" of other discourses and practices. And it is the emergence of the discourse on pedagogy — the discursive constitution of childhood — that I have attempted to outline through a description and explanation of the circumscribing conditions that led to its formation.

Turning now to discuss the value and implications of discursive history for a reconstruction of the child in history, the central methodological guide and substantive aim of this study has been to locate those intellectual and practical influences that converged in the construction of an institutionalized discourse that embodied a pedagogical model of the child.

Towards the end of the Middle Ages, European society was in a state of crisis. The political and economic reorganization of a largely undifferentiated population — the nonclerical, nonaristocratic common masses — is generally considered a central event in the development of modern European society. During the early modern era, organizing functions emerged through institutionalized forms such as police forces, prisons, charity hospitals for orphans, the elderly, and the sick, asylums for the mentally unstable, and schools for children. The corrective and disciplinary functions of these institutions were aimed at the normalization of the social body: to rehabilitate, improve, or make socially useful the unstable, the deviants, or the unschooled.

The establishment of schools enabled closer control over children who previously had received no specialized institutional treatment and had not been the object of specialized knowledge, but had been a largely heterogenous and unspecified population. Insofar as Luther and the moralists and pedagogues who followed his teachings, brought children as moral beings to the attention of adults, the rise of public and mandatory schooling, then, can be considered as one of the first institutions of morality, so to speak, that combined civil law with moral obligation, (legal) constraint with (spiritual) liberation, and the administration of knowledge with the administration of children.

In Foucault's work on criminality, mental illness, and sexuality, repression is viewed as a necessary historical counterpart of liberation, improvement, or rehabilitation. The birth of the school, then, like the birth of the prison, arose out of practical needs to cure (ignorance and moral depravity), to reform, to discipline, and to educate the social body. To institutionalize and secularize learning provided legal sanction for the state to control, train, punish and reward children who, hitherto, had been the private property of families, and not a part of the public, civil discourse. Foucault notes of the carceral that, "in its function, the power to punish is not essentially different from that of curing and educating."⁶ When applied to the school, the function of which was to cure ignorance, the consolidation of power to institutionalize children in the hands of the state, was, as we have seen, the only apparent alternative means to counteract not only the moral and spiritual deficiencies inherent in children, but to regulate and normalize childrearing. Having found parents generally unfit to teach the young, the reformers assumed that compulsory schooling would systematically mold and train young minds and bodies, and would individualize and equalize training in the context of enforced assembly of all children. Standardization of treatment — curricular content, rules, punishments, rewards — according to uniform codes was meant to preclude the idiosyncratic and unregulated moral training that families provided.

The school, then, like the prison, became the site of discursive practice, the practical expression of a discourse of both repression and formation: conformity and constraint to enable individual liberation, institutionalization of the whole to identify the singular subject, and rule systems of prohibition to delimit and expose subjects as objects of knowledge. Children's institutional confinement was meant to suppress sinful impulses, to censor immoral conduct, to delay the self-realization of sexual maturity; in short, to suspend the development of personal autonomy. The objective of this pedagogy of prohibition was to give children the tools for salvation: literacy for personal faith and redemption via scripture and for meaningful participation in the worldly estate, and self-discipline to combat the inevitable temptations to sin. The reformers assumed that parental neglect, laxity, or severity in early childrearing could be normalized through schooling where all children would be subject to the same educational treatment: knowledge, rules, and examinations. And here, printing overlapped with pedagogy through its organizing and standardizing function of providing multiple and identical texts and ordinances.

The pedagogical discourse that emerged out of early German Protestantism established children as a distinct social group and created public institutions for them in which to standardize their beliefs, behaviors, attitudes, and values. By bringing children and adolescents together under the rule of civil law, in buildings separate from the privacy of the home and public life in the streets, ruled by adults especially trained to teach, control, and observe large groups of children, and under the rule of written codes that prescribed, defined, and organized almost all aspects of school activities, a "culture of youth" was formed — visible and distinct from the social body.

Underlying the formation of this institutional discourse was an essentially negative concept of childhood, although the practices surrounding and attitudes advocated towards children should be seen — in the sixteenth century intellectual context — as positive efforts to counterbalance the negative first principle of innate sin. Advocacy of affection for children by parents and kind treatment by teachers, yet insistance on "rule by the rod" when necessary at home or at school, was meant to provide children with a balanced upbringing in which affection and discipline were to be meted out in equal measure. The reformers' concerns about children's vulnerability to their innate predispositions to sin and about children's defenselessness against parental neglect or indulgence, raised the problem of control for conformity. Children, easy victims or "prey for the devil," needed protection from the evil in themselves, and from the kind of moral corruption that pervaded society. A more totalized administration over society, one meant to inhibit political, social, and religious fragmentation, could be achieved by beginning with the young. By separating youth from adult society, knowledge input and output could be more broadly controlled by means of the school; schooling would facilitate the registration, supervision and certification of an important segment of society — the cognitively malleable and politically powerless. What appears to contemporary sensibility as repressive regimentation, schooling, as prescribed in the ordinances and visitation documents, seemed to sixteenth century Protestant reformers as a reasonable and well-intentioned means by which to save the individual from her or himself, and to save a disunified society in danger of complete and permanent disintegration.

That this pedagogical homogenization of one strata of the populace would generate its own forms of resistance was reflected in the continuation and, indeed, increase of school visitations during the second half of the sixteenth century when Melanchthon's humanistic *Instructions to the Visitors* had been transformed into a blueprint for persecution through what had become church-school inquisitions.[7] The upheavals in the church first instigated by Luther provided the impetus for the spiritual renewal of women and men, the restructuring of the social, the redistribution of real and symbolic power from ecclesiastical to secular authorities, and the setting of new aims for the individual and for society. The objectives of this spiritual and social renewal could best be met, in the estimation of the reformers, if successive generations were inspired and convinced of the importance, authenticity, and truth of God's words. Children needed to learn to read — and to read the same texts. The reformers believed that scripture contained in unambiguous terms the natural, divine laws of human rights, duties, and liberties that future generations would need to understand, protect and defend, and transmit to their offspring. And how else to embark on this program of social and spiritual renewal but systematically to lay its foundations in children and youth.

Notes

Introduction

1. P. Aries, *Centuries of Childhood: A Social History of Family Life*, trans. R. Baldick (New York: Alfred Knopf, 1962); D. Hunt, *Parents and Children in History* (New York: Basic Books, 1970); L. DeMause, ed., *The History of Childhood* (New York: The Psycho-history Press, 1974); E. Shorter, *The Making of the Modern Family* (New York: Basic Books, 1975).

2. L. Stone, *The Family, Sex and Marriage in England 1500-1800* (New York: Harper & Row, 1977); L. Stone, "Family History in the 1980s: Past Achievements and Future Trends," *The Journal of Interdisciplinary History*, 12 (1), 1981, pp. 51-87; L. Pollock, *Forgotten Children: Parent-Child Relations from 1500-1900* (New York: Cambridge University Press, 1983); G. Strauss, *Luther's House of Learning* (Baltimore: Johns Hopkins University Press, 1978); P. Greven, *The Protestant Temperament* (New York: Alfred Knopf, 1977); K. Wrightson, *English Society 1580-1680* (London: Hutchinson Social History of England, 1982).

3. For example: Aries, *Centuries of Childhood*; Shorter, *The Making of the Modern Family*; DeMause, *The History of Childhood*.

Chapter 1

1. Cf. Aries, *Centuries of Childhood*.

2. Ibid.

3. Stone, "Family History in the 1980s," p. 73.

4. M. Foucault, *The Birth of the Clinic, An Archaeology of Medical Perception*, trans. A. Sheridan Smith, (New York: Vintage Books, 1975) p. xix.

5. Cf. H. Innis, *The Bias of Communication* (Toronto: Toronto University Press, 1951).

6. See, for example, Strauss, *Luther's House of Learning* (Baltimore: Johns Hopkins University Press, 1978); Stone, *The Family, Sex and Marriage in England 1500-1800* (New York: Harper & Row, 1977); E. Eisenstein, *The Printing Press as an Agent of Change*, vols. 1 and 2 (New York: Cambridge University Press, 1980); M. McLuhan, *The Gutenberg Galaxy* (Toronto: University of Toronto Press, 1962).

7. L. Stone, *Past and Present* (Boston: Routledge & Kegan Paul, 1981) p. 102.

8. H. J. Chaytor, *From Script to Print* (London: Sidgwick & Jackson, 1966) p. 138.

9. See, for example: H. Graff, *Literacy and Social Development in the West* (Cambridge: Cambridge University Press, 1981); H. Graff, "Legacies of Literacy," *Journal of Communication*, 32 (1), 1982, 12-26; Eisenstein, *The Printing Press*; L. Febvre and H. J. Martin, *The Coming of the Book: The Impact of Printing 1450-1800*, trans. D. Gerard, G. Nowell-Smith and D. Wooten, eds., (Norfolk, U.K.: Lower & Brydone, 1976).

10. Eisenstein, *The Printing Press*, p. 28

11. M. Foucault, *Discipline and Punish: The Birth of the Prison*, trans. A. Sheridan Smith, (New York: Vintage Books, 1979); M. Foucault, *Madness and Civilization: A History of Insanity in the Age of Reason* (New York: Vintage Books, 1973); Foucault, *The Birth of the Clinic*.

12. Foucault, *Discipline and Punish*, p. 11

13. Ibid., p. 189.

14. Ibid., p. 147.

15. M. Foucault, *The Archaeology of Knowledge and the Discourse on Language*, trans. A. Sheridan Smith, (New York: Harper & Row, 1972) p. 219.

16. Ibid., p. 227.

17. R. D'Amico, "What is Discourse?" *Humanities in Society*, 5 (3 and 4), 1982, p. 210.

18. M. Foucault, "Questions of Method: An Interview," *Ideology and Consciousness*, 8, 1981, p. 8.

19. Ibid., p. 8.

20. Cf. V. Tufte, and B. Meyerhoff, eds., *Changing Images of the Family* (New Haven: Yale University Press, 1979); Stone, "Family History in the 1980s."

21. Graff, "Legacies of Literacy," *Literacy and Social Development*; D. Cressy, *Literacy and the Social Order: Reading and Writing*

in Tudor and Stuart England (Cambridge University Press, 1980); Eisenstein, *The Printing Press*; R. Gawthrop, "Literacy Drives in Pre-industrial Germany." In R. F. Arnove and H. Graff, eds., *National Literacy Campaigns* (New York: Plenum Press, 1987) pp. 29–48.

22. Cressy, *Literacy and the Social Order*, pp. 45–6.

23. H. Graff, *Literacy and History: An Interdisciplinary Research Bibliography*, rev. ed., (New York: Garland Press, 1981); Graff, "Legacies of Literacy," *Literacy and Social Development.* Overestimating the influence of print on cognitive processes and social organization is commonly attributed to McLuhan, *The Gutenberg Galaxy*.

24. F. Engels, *The Peasant War in Germany*, trans., M. J. Olgin, (New York: International Publishers, 1926).

25. See, for example, F. Braudel, *The Structures of Everyday Life*, trans. S. Reynolds, vol. 1 (New York: Harper & Row, 1979).

26. Stone, *Past and Present*, p. 101.

27. Aries, *Centuries of Childhood*; Stone, *Family, Sex and Marriage in England*.

28. Aries, *Centuries of Childhood*, p. 23.

29. Strauss, *Luther's House of Learning*, p. 554.

30. Aries, *Centuries of Childhood*, pp. 121, 128.

31. Ibid., p. 239.

32. Cf. Strauss, *Luther's House of Learning*, p. 355.

33. Aries, *Centuries of Childhood*, p. 239.

34. Ibid., p. 239.

35. Stone, *The Family, Sex and Marriage in England*, p. 99.

36. Ibid., pp. 101–2.

37. Cf. G. R. Elton, "Happy Families," *The New York Review of Books*, 14, June, 1984.

38. Stone, *The Family, Sex and Marriage in England*, p. 7.

39. Ibid., p. 8.

40. Cf. S. Ozment, *When Fathers Ruled: Family Life in Reformation Europe* (Cambridge: Harvard University Press, 1983).

41. Foucault, "Questions of Method," p. 8.

42. P. Laslett, *The Worlds We Have Lost*, 2d ed., (New York: Charles Scribner's Sons, 1973).

43. Aries, *Centuries of Childhood*, p. 125.

44. Cf. P. Aries, *The Hour of our Death*, trans. H. Weaver, (Harmondsworth, U.K.: Penguin, 1984).

45. Cf. J. Derrida, *Writing and Difference*, trans. A. Bass, (Chicago: Chicago University Press, 1978).

46. Laslett, *The Worlds We Have Lost*, p. 110.

47. Foucault, *The Archaeology*, p. 66.

48. J. Donzelot, *The Policing of Families*, trans. B. Hurley, (New York: Pantheon Books, 1979).

49. Foucault, *The Archaeology*, p. 66.

50. M. Foucault, "The History of Sexuality: Interview," *Oxford Literary Review*, 4 (2), 1980, p. 6.

Chapter 2

1. T. K. Haraven, "The History of the Family as an Interdisciplinary Field." In T. K. Rabb and R. F. Rotberg, eds., *The Family in History* (New York: Octagon Books, 1976).

2. Cf. L. Vogel, *Rummaging through the Primitive Past: A Note on Family Industrialization and Capitalism* (Chicago: Newberry Library, 1976).

3. Cf. M. Anderson, *Approaches to the History of the Western Family 1500-1914* (London: The Macmillan Press, 1980) p. 39; R. T. Vann, "Review Essay: The Family, Sex and Marriage in England 1500-1800," *Journal of Family History*, 4 (3), 1979, p. 300.

4. B. Hanawelt, "Childrearing Among the Lower Classes of Late Medieval England." In R. E. Rotberg and T. K. Rabb, eds., *Marriage and Fertility* (Princeton: Princeton University Press, 1980).

5. Aries, *Centuries of Childhood*, p. 128.

6. DeMause, *The History of Childhood*, p. 4.

7. Aries, *Centuries of Childhood*, p. 9.

8. Strauss, *Luther's House of Learning*, p. 331.

9. Aries, *Centuries of Childhood*, p. 262.

10. Anderson, *Approaches to the History of the Western Family*, p. 15.

11. Hanawelt, "Childrearing Among the Lower Classes," p. 29.

12. Cf. Vann, "Review Essay."

13. Ozment, *When Fathers Ruled*.

14. Pollock, *Forgotten Children*; See also review article by: J. R. Gillis, "Forgotten Children," *Journal of Indisciplinary History,* 16 (1), 1985, pp. 142–44.

15. E. Erikson, *Gandhi's Truth* (New York: W. W. Norton, 1969); E. Erikson, *Young Man Luther* (New York: W. W. Norton, 1958).

16. Hunt, *Parents and Children in History*; DeMause, *The History of Childhood*.

17. DeMause, *The History of Childhood*.

18. F. Halla, "Childhood, Culture and Society in Psychoanalysis and History," *The Historian*, 39 (3), 1977, p. 426.

19. B. Wishy, "Review Essay: Jung and Easily Freudened," *Journal of Family History*, 3 (1), 1978, p. 104.

20. DeMause, *The History of Childhood*, p. 3.

21. Hunt, *Parents and Children in History*.

22. DeMause, *The History of Childhood*, p. 32.

23. Anderson, *Approaches to the History of the Western Family*, p. 15.

24. Foucault, *The Archaeology*, p. 91.

25. Ibid., p. 45.

26. Ibid., p. 45.

27. Foucault, "The History of Sexuality: Interview".

28. DeMause, *The History of Childhood*, p. 1.

29. Ibid., p. 36.

30. Ibid., p. 38.

31. Ibid., p. i.

32. Wishy, "Review Essay," p. 104.

33. Foucault, *The Archaeology*, p. 22.

34. Wishy, "Review Essay," p. 103.

35. DeMause, *The History of Childhood*, p. 3.

36. P. Abrams, "History, Sociology, Historical Sociology," *Past and Present*, 87, 1980, p. 8.

37. DeMause, *The History of Childhood*, p. 3.

38. DeMause, *The History of Childhood*, p. 54.

39. Ibid., p. 54.

40. M. Foucault, *The Order of Things, An Archaeology of the Human Sciences* (New York: Vintage Books, 1973).

41. Foucault, *The Archaeology*, p. 8.

42. Ibid., p. 13.

43. DeMause, *The History of Childhood*, p. 54.

44. Wishy, "Review Essay," p. 105.

45. Hunt, *Parents and Children in History*, p. 7.

46. Ibid., p. 166.

47. Ibid., p. 166.

48. Anderson, *Approaches to the History of the Western Family*, p. 59.

49. Ibid., p. 36.

50. Ibid., p. 37.

51. See, for example: Laslett, *The Worlds We Have Lost*; J. L. Flandrin, *Families in Former Times,* trans. R. Southern, (London: Cambridge University Press, 1979); M. Spufford, "First Steps in

Literacy: The Reading and Writing Experiences of the Humblest Seventeenth-Century Spiritual Biographers." In Graff, *Literacy and Social Development in the West.*

52. Anderson, *Approaches to the History of the Western Family,* p. 34.

53. Ibid., p. 34.

54. Hanawelt, "Childrearing Among the Lower Classes."

55. Ibid., p. 28.

56. Ibid., p. 32.

57. Foucault, *The Archaeology,* p. 45.

58. Aries, *Centuries of Childhood,* p. 72-3.

59. Ibid., pp. 315-28.

60. Ibid., p. 368.

61. Ibid., p. 29.

62. Hunt, *Parents and Children in History,* p. 34.

63. See, for example: Pollock, *Forgotten Children*; Ozment, *When Fathers Ruled.*

64. Ibid.

65. Aries, *Centuries of Childhood,* p. 34.

66. Ibid., p. 34.

67. Eisenstein, *The Printing Press as an Agent of Change,* p. 33.

68. Aries, *Centuries of Childhood,* pp. 152-53.

69. Ibid., pp. 385-87.

70. Ibid., p. 397.

71. For informative reviews see: R. Baldick, "Centuries of Childhood: A Social History of Family Life," *History of Education Quarterly,* 4 (4), 1964, pp. 407-9; J. Thirsk, "The Family," *Past and Present,* 27, 1964, pp. 116-22; I. Q. Brown, "Philippe Aries on Education and Society in Seventeenth and Eighteenth Century France," *History of Education Quarterly,* 7 (4), 1967, pp. 357-68; Hunt, *Parents and Children in History*; I. Hardach-Pinke and G. Hardach, *Deutsche Kinderleben* (Regensburg, Germany: Athenaum Verlag, 1978); R. Wheaton and T. K. Hareven, eds., *The Family and Sexuality in French History* (Philadelphia: University of Pennsylvania Press, 1980). See also: Strauss, *Luther's House of Learning*; Stone, *The Family, Sex and Marriage in England*; Ozment, *When Fathers Ruled.*

72. Aries, *Centuries of Childhood,* pp. 412-13.

73. C. G. Nauert, "The Communications Revolution and Cultural Change," *The Sixteenth Century Journal,* 11 (1), 1980, p. 103.

74. Stone, *The Family, Sex and Marriage in England,* p. 123.

75. Foucault, *The Archaeology,* pp. 41-2.

76. Ibid., p. 42.
77. Ibid., p. 42.
78. Ibid., p. 44.
79. Febvre and Martin, *The Coming of the Book*, p. 248.
80. Ibid., pp. 260, 262.
81. Ibid., p. 288.
82. G. H. Putnam, *Books and their Makers During the Middle Ages*, vol. 2 (New York: Hilary House, (Originally published, 1896), 1962) p. 218.
83. Eisenstein, *The Printing Press as an Agent of Change*, p. 91.
84. Ibid., p. 88.
85. Putnam, *Books and Their Makers*, p. 439.
86. Ibid., p. 439.
87. Ibid., p. 443.
88. Febvre and Martin, *The Coming of the Book*, pp. 244–46.
89. Putnam, *Books and Their Makers*, p. 240.
90. Ibid., p. 241.
91. E. Eisenstein, "The Impact of Printing on European Education," In P. W. Musgrave, ed., *Sociology, History and Education* (London: Methuen, 1970) p. 89.
92. Nauert, "The Communications Revolution," p. 103.
93. Strauss, *Luther's House of Learning*, p. 336.
94. Ibid., p. 337.
95. Aries, *Centuries of Childhood*, p. 262.
96. Strauss, *Luther's House of Learning*, p. 355.

Chapter 3

1. Foucault, *Discipline and Punish*, p. 124.
2. Foucault, *Archaeology*, p. 28.
3. D'Amico, "What is Discourse?", p. 204.
4. F. Würtz, "Practica der Wund-Artzney." In Strauss, *Luther's House of Learning*, p. 89.
5. N. Levarie, *The Art and History of Books* (New York: James H. Heineman, 1968) p. 78.
6. E. Geck, *Johannes Gutenberg*. (Bad Godesberg: Internationes, 1968) p. 28.
7. W. T. Berry and H. E. Poole, *Annals of Printing* (Toronto: University of Toronto Press, 1966) p. 13.
8. Geck, *Johannes Gutenberg*, p. 44.
9. Ibid., p. 45.

10. Ibid., p. 47.

11. Ibid., p. 49.

12. Ibid., p. 50.

13. Ibid., p. 54.

14. J. Janssen, *History of the German People at the Close of the Middle Ages*, vol. 1 (New York: AMS Press, 1976) p. 14.

15. Berry and Poole, *Annals of Printing*, p. 73.

16. Geck, *Johannes Gutenberg*, p. 54.

17. Febvre and Martin, *The Coming of the Book*, p. 186.

18. Geck, *Johannes Gutenberg*, p. 54.

19. Ibid., p. 54.

20. Levarie, *Art and History of Books*, p. 105.

21. Ibid., pp. 180–82.

22. G. Strauss, *Nüremberg in the 16th Century* (New York: John Wiley, 1966).

23. Febvre and Martin, *The Coming of the Book*, p. 183.

24. Ibid., p. 320.

25. Ibid., p. 278.

26. J. Goody, *The Domestication of the Savage Mind* (New York: Cambridge University Press, 1977).

27. Febvre and Martin, *The Coming of the Book*, pp. 322–23.

28. Chaytor, *From Script to Print*, pp. 45–6.

29. R. Hirsch, *The Printed Word: Its Impact and Diffusion* (London: Variorum Reprints, 1976) p. 33.

30. Strauss, *Luther's House of Learning*, p. 343.

31. Ibid., p. 341.

32. Ibid., p. 149.

33. Elton, "Happy Families," p. 40.

34. M. Weber, *The Protestant Ethic and the Spirit of Capitalism*, trans. T. Parsons, (New York: Charles Scribner's Sons, (Originally published, 1904), 1958) p. 45.

35. Strauss, *Luther's House of Learning*, p. 346.

36. Ibid., p. 340.

37. Ibid., p. 345.

38. Ibid., p. 39.

39. Würtz, "Practica." In DeMause, *History of Childhood*, p. 39.

40. Strauss, *Luther's House of Learning*, p. 89.

41. Ibid., p. 89.

42. G. F. Still, *The History of Pediatrics* (Oxford: Oxford University Press, 1931) p. 86.

43. Ibid., p. 89.

44. Ibid., p. 94.

45. Ozment, *When Fathers Ruled*, p. 217.

46. Still, *History of Pediatrics*, p. 96.

47. Ibid., p. 94.

48. Ibid., p. 102.

49. Strauss, *Luther's House of Learning*, p. 88.

50. M. Luther, "On the Estate of Marriage." In W. Brandt, ed., *Luther's Works*, vol. 45 (Philadelphia: Muhlenberg Press, (Originally published, 1522), 1962) p. 40.

51. M. Hanneman, *The Diffusion of the Reformation in South-Western Germany, 1518—1534* (Chicago: Department of Geography, University of Chicago, 1975) p. 59.

52. Ibid., p. 22.

53. Strauss, *Luther's House of Learning*, p. 193.

54. R. G. Cole, "The Dynamics of Printing in the Sixteenth Century." In L. Buck and J. Zophy, eds., *The Social History of the Reformation* (Columbus: Ohio State University Press, 1972) p. 97.

55. Cf. Chaytor, *From Script to Print*.

56. Geck, *Johannes Gutenberg*, p. 58.

57. Febvre and Martin, *The Coming of the Book*, p. 188.

58. Ibid., p. 192.

59. Ibid., p. 192.

60. Ibid., p. 289.

61. Putnam, *Books and Their Makers*, p. 221.

62. Febvre and Martin, *The Coming of the Book*, p. 289.

63. Putnam, *Books and Their Makers*, p. 220.

64. Ibid., p. 225.

65. Febvre and Martin, *The Coming of the Book*, p. 294.

66. Ibid., p. 295.

67. Ibid., p. 294.

68. Putnam, *Books and Their Makers*, pp. 223-24.

69. From school visitation instructions cited in Strauss, *Luther's House of Learning*, p. 131.

70. Ibid., p. 131.

71. Ibid., p. 127.

72. McLuhan, *Gutenberg Galaxy*.

73. H. Holborn, *A History of Modern Germany* (New York: Alfred Knopf, 1961) p. 37.

74. P. Blickle, *The Revolution of 1525*, trans. T. Brady Jr. and H. Midelfort, (Baltimore: Johns Hopkins University Press, 1981) p. 77.

75. Cf. Braudel, *Structures of Everyday Life*, p. 51.

76. Cf. C. Cipolla, *Before the Industrial Revolution: European Society and Economy, 1000-1700*, 2d ed., (New York: W. W. Norton, 1980).

77. Braudel, F. *The Wheels of Commerce*, trans. S. Reynolds, vol. 2 (New York: Harper & Row, 1982), p. 418.

78. Ibid., p. 418.

79. Blickle, *The Revolution of 1525*, p. 65.

80. Ibid., p. 18.

81. Ibid., p. 22.

82. Ibid., p. xxi.

83. Holborn, *History of Modern Germany*, p. 183.

Chapter 4

1. The Instructions are commonly cited in biographies of Melanchthon and Luther without publication details. Two primary source references are cited in Strauss, *Luther's House of Learning*, pp. 321, 316; See also: R. Stupperich, *Melanchthon's Werke in Auswahl* (Germany: Gütersloh, 1951); and *Dr. Martin Luther's Werke: Kritische Gesamtausgabe* (Germay: Weimar (Originally published, 1883; reprinted 1964-8).

2. Strauss, *Luther's House of Learning*, p. 268-90.

3. Eby and Arrowood. *The Development of Modern Education*, p. 84.

4. Ibid., p. 84.

5. M. Luther, "An Answer to Several Questions on Monastic Vows." In R. Schultz trans. and ed., *Luther's Works*, vol. 46 (Philadelphia: Fortress Press, (Originally published, 1526), 1967) p. 149.

6. M. Luther, "Address to the Christian Nobility of the German Nation Respecting the Reformation of the Christian Estate," trans. C. Bucheim. In *Harvard Classics*, vol. 36 (New York: Collier & Sons, (Originally published, 1520), 1910) p. 338.

7. M. Luther, "A Sermon on Keeping Children in School." In C. Jacobs, trans. and R. Schultz, ed., *Luther's Works*, vol. 46 (Philadelphia: Fortress Press, (Originally published, 1530), 1967) p. 215.

8. Luther, "Address to the Christian Nobility," p. 339.

9. M. Luther, "Admonition to Peace: A Reply to the Twelve Articles of the Peasants in Swabia." In C. Jacobs, trans. and R. Schultz, ed., *Luther's Works*, vol. 54 (Philadelphia: Fortress Press, (Originally published, 1525), 1967) p. 39.

10. Luther, "A Sermon on Keeping Children in School," p. 250.

11. Ibid., p. 251.

12. Eby and Arrowood, *The Development of Modern Education*, p. 87.

13. Ibid., p. 88; O. Thulin, *A Life of Luther* (Philadelphia: Fortress Press, 1966) p. 104.

14. Thulin, *A Life of Luther*, p. 104.

15. S. C. Parker, *The History of Modern Elementary Education* (New York: Ginn and Company, 1912) p. 50.

16. Ibid., p. 52.

17. Cf. for example: Thulin, *Life of Luther*; Eby, *Early Protestant Educators*; Fromm, *Young Man Luther*.

18. Eby and Arrowood, *Development of Modern Education*, p. 92.

19. W. Goodsell, *A History of Marriage and the Family* (New York: MacMillan, 1935) p. 267.

20. Luther, "Address to the Christian Nobility," p. 317.

21. Cited in R. Bainton, *Women of the Reformation in Germany and Italy* (Minneapolis: Augsburg Publishing House, 1971) p. 34.

22. Ibid., p. 42.

23. Strauss, *Luther's House of Learning*, p. 90.

24. Cf. Ozment, *When Fathers Ruled*, pp. 167–68.

25. Bainton, *Women of the Reformation*, p. 81.

26. Cited in Bainton, *Women of the Reformation*, p. 84.

27. Stupperich, *Melanchthon*, p. 62.

28. Cited in Bainton, *Women of the Reformation*, p. 32.

29. Cited in Strauss, *Luther's House of Learning*, p. 90.

30. Cited in Strauss, *Luther's House of Learning*, p. 124.

31. Ibid., p. 99.

32. Cited in Strauss, *Luther's House of Learning*, p. 99.

33. Cited in Strauss, *Luther's House of Learning*, p. 100.

34. St. Augustine, *The Confessions*, E. B. Pusey, trans. and C. W. Eliot, ed., In *Harvard Classics*, vol. 7 (New York: Collier & Sons, 397–8 C.E./1909) p. 11.

35. Ibid., pp. 176–77.

36. Ibid., p. 13.

37. Ibid., p. 14.

38. St. Augustine, *The Confessions*, trans. R. S. Coffin, (Harmondsworth: Penguin, 1961) p. 28.

39. Foucault, *Archaeology*, p. 46.

40. M. Foucault, *Language, Counter-Memory, Practice*, ed. D. F. Bouchard, and D. F. Bouchard and S. Simon, trans., (Ithaca, New York: Cornell University Press, 1977) p. 138.

41. M. Poster, *Foucault, Marxism, and History* (Oxford: Blackwell, 1984) p. 89.

42. Strauss, *Luther's House of Learning*, p. 54.

43. Cf. Stone, *Family, Sex and Marriage in England*, p. 92.

44. Strauss, *Luther's House of Learning*, p. 54.

45. Cf. C. Lucas, *Our Western Educational Heritage* (New York: Macmillan, 1972).

46. M. Luther, "Every Seventh Year Brings a Change, From 'Table Talk Collected by Conrad Cordatus.'" In T. Tappert, trans. and ed., *Luther's Works*, vol. 54 (Philadelphia: Fortress Press, (Originally published, 1532), 1967) p. 190.

47. St. Augustine, *The Confessions*, p. 23.

48. Ibid., p. 23.

49. Strauss, *Luther's House of Learning*, p. 55.

50. M. Luther, "Girls Grow Up More Quickly Than Boys, From 'Table Talk Collected by Conrad Cordatus.'" In T. Tappert, trans. and ed., *Luther's Works*, vol. 54 (Philadelphia: Fortress Press, (Originally published, 1533), 1967) p. 187.

51. Strauss, *Luther's House of Learning*, p. 323.

52. Cited in Strauss, *Luther's House of Learning*, p. 55.

53. Ibid., p. 55.

54. M. Luther, "Examples of the Faulty Proofs of the Papists, From 'Table Talk Recorded by Anthony Lauterbach.'" In T. Tappert, trans. and ed., *Luther's Works*, vol. 54 (Philadelphia: Fortress Press, (Originally published, 1538), 1967) p. 324.

55. Cited in Strauss, *Luther's House of Learning*, p. 102.

56. Luther, "Answer to Several Questions on Monastic Vows," p. 147.

57. Strauss, *Luther's House of Learning*, p. 103.

58. J. L. Flandrin, "Repression and Change in the Sexual Life of Young People in Medieval and Early Modern Times." In R. Wheaton and T. K. Hareven, eds., *Family and Sexuality in French History* (Philadelphia: University of Pennsylvania Press, 1980) p. 29.

59. L. Stone, ed., *Schooling and Society* (Baltimore: Johns Hopkins University Press, 1976) p. xii.

60. Cited in C. Manschreck, *Melanchthon* (New York: Abington Press, 1958) p. 155.

61. Ibid., p. 204.

62. Strauss, *Luther's House of Learning*, p. 105.

63. Ibid., p. 204.

64. Cited in Goodsell, *History of Marriage and the Family*, p. 296.

65. Cited in Goodsell, *History of Marriage and the Family*, p. 297.

66. Ibid., p. 297.

67. Cited in J. Janssen, *A History of the German People at the Close of the Middle Ages*, vol. 1 (New York: AMS Press, 1966) p. 31.

68. Cited in Janssen, *History of the German People at the Close of the Middle Ages*, p. 25.

69. Ibid., p. 25.

70. Cited in Eby, *Early Protestant Educators*, pp. 54-5.

71. Cited in Eby, *Early Protestant Educators*, p. 53.

72. Ibid., p. 53.

73. Cited in R. Ulich, *A History of Religious Education: Documents and Interpretations from the Judaeo-Christian Tradition* (New York: New York University Press, 1968) p. 248.

74. W. Learned, *The Oberlehrer: A Study of the Social and Professional Evolution of the German Schoolmaster* (Cambridge: Harvard University Press, 1914) pp. 14–22.

75. Stone, *Family, Sex and Marriage in England*, p. xii.

76. Strauss, *Luther's House of Learning*, p. 251.

77. Cited in Eby, *Early Protestant Educators*, pp. 24–5.

78. Cited in Eby, *Early Protestant Educators*, p. 27.

79. Ibid., p. 27.

80. Cited in Eby, *Early Protestant Educators*, p. 34.

81. Ibid., p. 34.

82. Cited in Eby, *Early Protestant Educators* p. 24.

83. Cited in Eby, *Early Protestant Educators*, p. 25.

Chapter 5

1. Arnove and Graff, *National Literacy Campaigns*, p. 6.

2. Gawthrop, "Literacy Drives in Preindustrial Germany," p. 31.

3. Strauss, *Luther's House of Learning*.

4. W. H. Woodward, *Studies in Education During the Age of the Renaissance, 1400–1600* (New York: Russell and Russell, 1965) p. 219.

5. Eby and Arrowood, *The Development of Modern Education*, p. 222.

6. Woodward, *Studies in Education During the Renaissance*, p. 222.

7. Eby and Arrowood, *The Development of Modern Education*, p. 102.

8. Woodward, *Studies in Education During the Renaissance*, p. 222.

9. F. Painter, *A History of Education* (New York: Appleton and Company, 1980), p. 167.

10. Woodward, *Studies in Education During the Renaissance*, p. 219.

11. J. Mackinnon. *Luther and the Reformation*, vol. 4 (New York: Russell and Russell, 1962) p. 102.

12. Ibid., p. 102.

13. Cf. Chaytor, *From Script to Print*; McLuhan, *The Gutenberg Galaxy*.

14. Cited in Eby, *Early Protestant Educators*, p. 165.

15. Ibid., p. 165.

16. Woodward, *Studies in Education During the Renaissance*, p. 220.

17. Ibid., p. 220.

18. Ibid., p. 221.

19. Cited in Eby, *Early Protestant Educators*, p. 213.

20. Ibid., p. 213.

21. Ibid., p. 224.

22. Ibid., pp. 244–45.

23. Ibid., p. 225.

24. Ibid., p. 225.

25. Ibid., pp. 225–26.

26. Ibid., p. 226.

27. Ibid., p. 226.

28. Ibid., p. 226.

29. Ibid., p. 220.

30. Ibid., p. 201.

31. Foucault, *Discipline and Punish*, p. 161.

32. Ibid., p. 161.

33. Ibid., pp. 161–62.

34. Ibid., p. 152.

35. Cf. Strauss, *Luther's House of Learning*.

36. Cf. Foucault, *Discipline and Punish*.

37. Ibid., p. 187.

38. P. Rabinow, ed., *The Foucault Reader* (Harmondsworth: Peregrine, 1986) p. 8.

39. Learned, *The Oberlehrer*, p. 17.

40. Gawthrop, "Literacy Drives in Preindustrial Germany," p. 33.

41. Learned, *The Oberlehrer*, p. 17.

42. Cf. Gawthrop, *"Literacy Drives in Preindustrial Germany."*

43. Foucault, *Discipline and Punish*, p. 189.

44. Ibid., p. 187.

45. Ibid., p. 187.

46. Learned, *The Oberlehrer*, p. 20.

47. Foucault, *Discipline and Punish*, p. 179.

48. Ibid., p. 179.

49. Ibid., p. 189.

50. Luther, "Address to the Christian Nobility," p. 232.

51. Cited in Parker, *History of Modern Elementary Education*, p. 50.

52. Cited in Strauss, *Luther's House of Learning*, p. 20.

53. Cited in Mackinnon, *Luther and the Reformation*, pp. 220–21.

54. Eby, *Early Protestant Educators*, p. 192.

55. Ibid., p. 192.

56. Cited in Eby, *Early Protestant Educators*, p. 204.

57. Ibid., p. 205.

58. Ibid., p. 205.

59. Ibid., p. 205.

60. Ibid., p. 212.

61. Ibid., p. 224.

62. Foucault, *Discipline and Punish*, p. 23.

63. Cf. J. Goody and I. Watt, "The Consequences of Literacy." In J. Goody, ed., *Literacy in Traditional Societies* (Cambridge: Cambridge University Press, 1968).

64. Cressy, *Literacy and the Social Order*, pp. 184–85.

65. Cited in Eby, *Early Protestant Educators*, p. 215.

66. Ibid., p. 215.

67. Ibid., p. 215.

68. Gawthrop, "Literacy Drives in Preindustrial Germany," p. 33.

69. Cited in Eby, *Early Protestant Educators*, p. 220.

70. Ibid., p. 222.

71. Foucault, *Discipline and Punish*, p. 211.

72. Cited in Eby, *Early Protestant Educators*, p. 223.

73. Cf. Holborn, *History of Modern Germany*.

74. Foucault, *Discipline and Punish*, p. 186.

75. Ibid., p. 191.

76. Ibid., p. 191.

77. Ibid., p. 187.

78. Ibid., p. 189.

79. Ibid., p. 191.

80. Ibid., p. 194.

81. Cressy, *Literacy and the Social Order*.

82. Cf. S. DeCastell and A. Luke, "Defining Literacy in North American Schools: Social and Historical Conditions and Consequences." *Journal of Curriculum Studies*, 15 (4), 1983 pp. 373–89; Graff, *Literacy and Social Development*.

Chapter 6

1. Febvre and Martin, *The Coming of the Book*, p. 288.

2. Eisenstein, *The Printing Press*, p. 432.

3. Foucault, *The Order of Things*.

4. Aries, *Centuries of Childhood*, p. 412
5. Foucault, *The Archaeology*, p. 7.
6. Foucault, *Discipline and Punish*, p. 303.
7. Cf. Strauss, *Luther's House of Learning*.

Index